T0294859

The Small Museum Toolkit, Book 3

The Small Museum Toolkit, Book 3

Organizational Management

Edited by
Cinnamon Catlin-Legutko
and Stacy Klingler

ALTAMIRA
PRESS

A division of
ROWMAN & LITTLEFIELD PUBLISHERS, INC.
Lanham • New York • Toronto • Plymouth, UK

Published by AltaMira Press
A division of Rowman & Littlefield Publishers, Inc.
A wholly owned subsidary of The Rowman & Littlefield Publishing Group, Inc.
4501 Forbes Boulevard, Suite 200, Lanham, Maryland 20706
http://www.altamirapress.com

Estover Road, Plymouth PL6 7PY, United Kingdom

British Library Cataloguing in Publication Information Available

Library of Congress Cataloging-in-Publication Data
The small museum toolkit. Book 3, Organizational management / edited by Cinnamon Catlin-Legutko and Stacy Klingler.
    p. cm. — (American Association for State and Local History book series)
  Includes bibliographical references and index.
  ISBN 978-0-7591-1950-5 (cloth : alk. paper) — ISBN 978-0-7591-1337-4 (pbk. : alk. paper) — ISBN 978-0-7591-1344-2 (electronic)
  1. Small museums—Personnel management. I. Catlin-Legutko, Cinnamon. II. Klingler, Stacy, 1976– III. Title: Organizational management.
  AM121.S634 2012
  069'.63—dc23   2011028451

∞™ The paper used in this publication meets the minimum requirements of American National Standard for Information Sciences—Permanence of Paper for Printed Library Materials, ANSI/NISO Z39.48-1992.

Printed in the United States of America

CONTENTS

EDITORS' NOTE

Small museums are faced with the enormous task of matching the responsibilities of a large museum—planning strategically, securing and managing human and financial resources, providing stewardship of collections (including historic buildings) as well as excellent exhibitions, programs, and publications, and responding to changing community and visitor needs—all with more limited human and financial resources. Small museum staff (paid or unpaid) often fulfill key responsibilities outside their area of expertise or training.

We recognize that small museum staff lack time more than anything. To help you in the trenches, we offer this quick reference, written with your working environment in mind, to make the process of becoming a sustainable, valued institution less overwhelming.

The Small Museum Toolkit is designed as a single collection of short, readable books that provides the starting point for realizing key responsibilities in museum work. Each book stands alone, but as a collection they represent a single resource to jump-start the process of pursing best practices and meeting museum standards.

If you are new to working in museums, you may want to read the entire series to get the lay of the land—an overview of what issues you should be aware of and where you can find resources for more information. If you have some museum training but are now responsible for more elements of museum operations than in your previous position, you may start with just the books or chapters covering unfamiliar territory. (You might be wishing you had taken a class in fundraising right about now!) As you prepare to tackle new challenges, we hope that you will refer back to a chapter to orient yourself.

While any chapter can be helpful if read in isolation, we suggest that you start with the first book, *Leadership, Mission, and Governance*, and look at the issues of mission, planning, and assessment. You will find that almost every chapter asks you to consider its subject in light of your mission and make decisions based on it. As you begin to feel overwhelmed by all the possible opportunities and challenges you face, assessment and planning will help you focus your scarce resources strategically—where you need them the most and where they can produce the biggest impact on your organization. And this book offers tips for good governance—defining the role of a trustee and managing the director-trustee relationship. Understanding this relationship from the outset will prevent many headaches down the road.

Financial Resource Development and Management offers you direction about how to raise and manage money and stay within your legal boundaries as a nonprofit. How to manage resources, human and inanimate, effectively and efficiently is discussed in *Organizational Management. Reaching and Responding to the Audience* encourages you to examine your museum audiences and make them comfortable, program to their needs and interests, and spread the word about your good work.

The remaining two books explore the museum foundational concepts of interpretation and stewardship in a small museum setting. *Interpretation: Education, Programs, and Exhibits* considers researching and designing exhibits and best practices for sharing the stories with your audiences. *Stewardship: Collections and Historic Preservation* rounds out the six-book series with an in-depth look at collections care, management, and planning.

We would like to thank the staff at the American Association for State and Local History and AltaMira Press, our families, and our colleagues for encouraging us to pursue this project. You have tirelessly offered your support, and we are incredibly grateful.

There is little reward for writing in service to the museum field—and even less time to do it when you work in a small museum. The contributors to this series generously carved time out of their work and personal lives to share with you their perspectives and lessons learned from years of experience. While not all of them currently hang their hats in small museums, every one of them has worked with or for a small museum and values the incredible work small museums accomplish every day. We offer each and every one of them more appreciation than we can put into words.

We hope that this series makes your lives—as small museum directors, board members, and paid and unpaid staff members—just a little bit easier. We hope that we have gathered helpful perspectives and pointed you in the direction of useful resources.

And when you are faced with a minor annoyance, a major disaster, or just one too many surprises, remember why you do this important work and that you are not alone.

It takes a very special kind of person to endure and enjoy this profession for a lifetime. Not a day passes in which I do not learn something, or find something, or teach something, or preserve something, or help someone.

—Unknown author

Keep up the good work!

Cinnamon Catlin-Legutko
Stacy Lynn Klingler
Editors

PREFACE

I have a confession to make. Until I got to the American Association for State and Local History (AASLH), I never truly understood what it was to work in a small museum. Sure, I had been around them, visited them, talked to my peers who worked in them both as paid and unpaid (read: volunteer) staff, and appreciated the role they play in the historical narrative and in communities. But I never *got it* until I got to AASLH.

So what have I learned? First and foremost, small museums are the bedrock of the American museum profession. You will not find museums the size of the Smithsonian or historic sites like Gettysburg in every American community, but you will often find a small museum, sometimes more than one. While we in the historical profession talk often about how we are the keepers of the American past, and we are, those who work in the smaller institutions are truly minders of our nation's patrimony and heritage. They care for the objects and history of communities throughout the country, stories that would probably be lost without that care. Quite simply, without small museums, our knowledge of the past, our historical narrative, would be incomplete.

The second thing I have learned, and been truly humbled by, is the passion and dedication small museum professionals and volunteers have for their craft. You will rarely hear small museum professionals complaining about a lack of resources—that is just part and parcel of the task at hand. Instead of attacking a challenge with reasons for why something cannot be done, they redirect their thoughts to how it can be done within the parameters provided. So, small museum professionals are equally comfortable with answering the phone, giving a tour, processing collections, and plunging the occasional toilet (the latter falling into the "other duties as assigned" category in a job description).

And amid all that, small museum professionals keep a great sense of humor. At several gatherings of small museum folks over the years, we have had fun with a game we call "You Know You Work in a Small Museum If . . ." Responses ranged from "A staff meeting consists of all staff members turning around in their office chairs at the same time" to "You're the director, but if you're the first one to work after a snowstorm, you get to shovel the sidewalk and plow the parking lot." But my absolute favorite was "When you walk through the gallery and hear a guest say, 'The staff should really do . . .' and you think, Hey, *I'm* my staff!"

At one time, as Steve Friesen of the Buffalo Bill Museum and Grave notes in chapter 2 of Book 1 of this series, the term *small museum* was used as a pejorative. Small museums were underfunded, under-resourced, and poorly managed. "If they weren't," the thinking went, "they'd be large museums, right?" Wrong. Being small does not mean you aspire to be big or that the institution is small because it is doing something wrong. Smallness has more to do with a spirit and dedication to a certain niche of history, a community, a person, a subject.

I believe the field has moved beyond that prejudice, and small museums are now celebrated. At AASLH we often discuss how much larger museums can learn from smaller institutions about how to serve as effective stewards of their resources and to engage their communities in a deep, meaningful way. There is much to learn from small museums, and our peers and colleagues at those institutions are ever willing to share.

Along this line, I have always found that one of the best things about the museum profession in general is how open it is with regard to sharing ideas and processes and just offering support. In no corner of the field is this more evident than in the world of small museums. Small museum professionals are founts of wisdom and expertise, and every small museum session, luncheon, or affinity event I have been to has been packed, and discussion has been stimulating and often inspiring. In fact, discussion often spills out into the hallways after the formal session has concluded.

But the work I know best is that of the AASLH Small Museums Committee. The editors of this series, Cinnamon Catlin-Legutko and Stacy Klingler, are, respectively, the founding and current chairs of this committee. Under their leadership, a team of small museum folks has completed a set of ambitious goals, including gathering a variety of research and developing a small museum needs assessment, presenting sessions at conferences throughout the country, and raising money for scholarships to send peers to the AASLH annual meeting each year. It is this last item I want to highlight as it gives the clearest example of the love and commitment those in small museums have for each other.

In my view, the fact that the Small Museums Committee successfully organizes an annual fundraising campaign is commendable. The fact that it routinely raises money to send *two* people to the meeting (and four people in some years) is truly remarkable. This is indicative of the passion and dedication small museum professionals feel toward the cause of small museums and toward their colleagues. Let's face it, history professionals are not at the top of the salary food chain. (I always note this whenever I speak to history classes about a career in public history. "If you choose this career, you are going to love what you do; you are going to be making a difference in your community. But you are also taking a vow of poverty. No one goes into the history field to get rich.") And while donors to this fund are not all from small museums, small museum professionals are a large part of the pool, giving as generously as anyone. I am so heartened each year as we raise this money.

So, what does all this have to do with the book in your hands? I would say a lot. First, the contributors are small museum professionals or aficionados themselves. They are dedicated to the craft in the small museum environment and know firsthand its needs and challenges. In addition, they have been involved with, and led national discussions on, these issues. They are passionate about the cause of small museums, and they have organized and written a book (and series) that offers a variety of voices and contexts while speaking to the needs as articulated. The thirty-plus contributors to this series offer a wealth of experience and expertise in dealing with the complex nature of running a small museum, in preserving traces of the American past for future generations, often on a shoestring budget and with limited resources. It is a lesson we can all learn. And it is a lesson well articulated here.

Whether you are a seasoned small museum professional, a newly minted executive director, or a museum studies or public history student, it is my hope that this book series will give you the tools you need to succeed in your job. I also hope that you will continue to carry the torch for small museums in your community and in the larger museum field. The field needs your passion and expertise, and the role you fill in your community is critical.

Bob Beatty
Vice President, AASLH

CAN YOU HAND ME THAT WRENCH?
MANAGING MUSEUM OPERATIONS

Claudia J. Nicholson

Are you new to managing a small museum? I bet you feel comfortable with your area(s) of expertise, but managing a facility might not be a part of your life or work experiences. Museum operations encompasses responsibility for the maintenance of your structure, the safety of your visitors, and the security of your staff and collections. It can initially be very daunting, and the stakes seem very high.

However, the job of managing museum operations is rewarding and involves common sense, backed by good policy and procedures, calendars, and schedules. Policy is the map, but procedures, calendars, and schedules are the step-by-step driving directions that will get you where you want to go. And there is a great deal of help to be had, from museum professionals, tradesmen, pest control specialists, and colleagues in other small museums. Very little of the advice here is exclusive to museums.

For the purposes of this chapter, the word "staff" refers to anyone, paid or unpaid, who works for your museum on a regular basis. The word "volunteer" refers to someone who works seasonally or more occasionally for you.

Managing a facility takes person-power—people who are willing to see to lawn mowing, snow shoveling, filter changing, and a host of other tasks related to taking care of a public building. There are individuals in the community who are willing to take these tasks on—you just need to find them.

First, let us consider your facility. Even if not a historic structure, it, along with your grounds, constitutes the single largest artifact for which you are responsible. To a certain extent, you cannot go wrong treating it like an artifact. In this chapter, I discuss the basics of facilities management, including putting someone in charge, writing things down, performing preventive and cyclical maintenance, monitoring for bugs (and other pests), and implementing green building systems.

Security and safety follows. Just as you should strive to maintain a safe environment for your collection, you must maintain a safe environment for your staff and visitors. I explain how good security need not be expensive or labor intensive, and I identify policies you should have and use to ensure visitor safety.

That leads us to insurance, as impenetrable and unnerving as it seems. Remember, insurance companies are your allies—they no more want to pay a claim than you want to make one. I go over all required insurance and discuss your options when it comes to collections insurance, directors and officers (D&O) insurance, and fine arts insurance for incoming or outgoing loans.

Finally, I discuss facility rental both as an opportunity to extend your mission into the community and as an income-generating activity. Rental activity involves pleasures as well as pitfalls, and I try to give you the tools to decide if facility rental is right for your organization.

Every activity you undertake depends on how well you take care of museum operations. I hope to make these crucial tasks seem less onerous.

Facility

Like it or not, your institution will be judged by how well it maintains its facilities and grounds. The neighbors will appreciate it if you keep the lawn mowed, your visitors will appreciate it if your parking lot is cleared after a snowfall and your restrooms do not smell, and your insurance carrier will be pleased to see that you have not blocked fire exits, that you have staff trained in the use of fire extinguishers, and that wet floors are blocked off so no one slips.

The essential ingredients of a well-managed and -maintained facility are few but critical. They include a facilities manager, an operations manual, plans for grounds keeping and regular cleaning, a commitment to preventive maintenance, and an integrated pest management (IPM) program. Your recipe for success is a board-reviewed and -approved policy that everyone follows.

Facility Manager

Someone must take responsibility for this task, but the organization may find that it takes up a great deal of the director's time. The facilities manager can be paid or unpaid. Of more importance is a willingness to put in the time necessary to ensure that your facility is well run.

The facilities manager is your key person in maintaining the safety and security of your facility. The work that he or she does, or causes to be done, will minimize accident, injury, damage, theft, and catastrophic loss. This individual will be very high up on the call list (second only to the director or board president) in the museum's disaster plan.

The facilities manager has a number of responsibilities, each of which must be seen to week after week, year after year. This person knows the building better than anyone else, has been in all the closets, rooms, attics, and basements, has walked the grounds, looking both down and up. The facilities manager knows the heating, ventilating, and air conditioning (HVAC) system and has been on the roof. That detailed knowledge of the facility will come in very handy when an alarm goes off unexpectedly or you suddenly find drip lines where there were none before. The facilities manager will either be directly responsible or delegate responsibility for cyclical and regular maintenance, grounds keeping, and the care of every building or outbuilding on your property. He or she will know the flora and fauna on your property. The facilities manager is also the keeper of the operations manual.

Operations Manual

If you do not have something like an operations manual at your facility now, then you and your facilities manager should begin assembling one immediately. (I inherited my building from the county with nothing but a set of original architectural drawings.) If precious little material exists to get you started, begin by documenting what the facilities manager is doing or having done. Knowing exactly when lightbulbs get changed (and approximately how many hours you get out of them) will, in the end, give you an excellent idea of your building's life cycle. This documentation will tell you when regular maintenance needs to occur and what tasks need doing at the change of seasons. (See textbox 1.1 for a list of suggested contents for an operations manual.) Record everything, even the seemingly unimportant items—it is impossible to know immediately upon occupying a new (to you) building where everything is or what everything represents. At some point, you will identify the spigot for which you have found the water shutoff.

In addition to the basics, you may wish to include things like environmental readings taken from data loggers or hygrothermographs, periodic light-level readings, floor-load information, and elevator sizes and load capacities. In fact, if you and your facilities manager have time to fill out the American Association of Museums (AAM) Registrars Committee's *General Facilities Report* (see the resource section at the end of the chapter), you will have a great deal of vital information about your facility all in one place.

Be sure to keep your operations manual up to date. Any time you have major work done at your facility, make sure that you gather all this important information and place it in the operations manual, purging superseded information. Review your operations manual yearly with your facilities manager to ensure that it has all the information you need.

OPERATIONS MANUAL SUGGESTED CONTENTS

The following items would be a great start for a basic operations manual:

- As-built drawings of the building
- Building map (floor plan)
  - Lighting map
  - Alarm map
  - All rooms with numbers or names
  - Circuit map (detailing which circuit breakers control which outlets and lights)
  - Plumbing map or information about the locations of shutoff valves
  - Fire-suppression system map
- Major modification or renovation description and drawings
- Basic maintenance schedule of building and grounds
  - Daily cleaning
  - Weekly cleaning
  - Monthly cleaning
  - Deep cleaning schedule
  - Filter change in HVAC system
  - Periodic tree-trimming and gutter-cleaning schedule
  - Major grounds keeping activities, such as fertilization, annual plantings, leaf removal
- Material safety datasheets for all chemicals used in the building
- Warranty or purchase records for building tools and equipment
- Manuals or other operating information for the museum's HVAC system
- Contact and contract information for vendors who regularly service the building
- Key and alarm code policy and current key log
- Notes on discoveries that the facilities manager has made

Grounds Keeping

First impressions are so important. As visitors to your institution first see your grounds, you need to ensure that they are in top condition at all times. Exterior tasks are divided into two major types: regular maintenance and periodic maintenance.

Photo 1.1. At the North Star Museum of Boy Scouting and Girl Scouting, the Facility Manager's office is called the "Bat Cave." Thus the *Bat Cave Notebooks* **comprise the museum's operations manual, painstakingly assembled since we moved into the building in 2005. It contains information on the building systems and equipment, discoveries made by the facilities manager, and the operating manuals for everything we use. The** *Maintenance Projects* **notebook contains information on all of the building projects undertaken, including a schedule of materials and techniques used to carry out the projects. It is an invaluable tool. (Courtesy of North Star Museum of Boy Scouting and Girl Scouting)**

Regular maintenance tasks are easy to identify—sweeping sidewalks, raking leaves, mowing grass, maintaining gardens, plowing parking lots, and clearing snow and ice from walkways. We all know what these are, and chances are good that anyone who runs a public building keeps up with them pretty well. The public needs to get in safely and take away the impression that you care about your building and grounds. Some of these things are also critical parts of risk management, which will be addressed later in the chapter.

You can get these regular tasks done in a number of ways. Daily sweeping or policing of the grounds can be performed by regular staff. Individuals who need to complete court-mandated community service or retired senior volunteers might be able to do some of this work. The same holds for lawn mowing, leaf raking, spring cleaning, and snow shoveling. Parking lot plowing is fairly specialized and sometimes will require you to hire a professional, depending on the size of your lot and other factors. A snow-removal company may consider

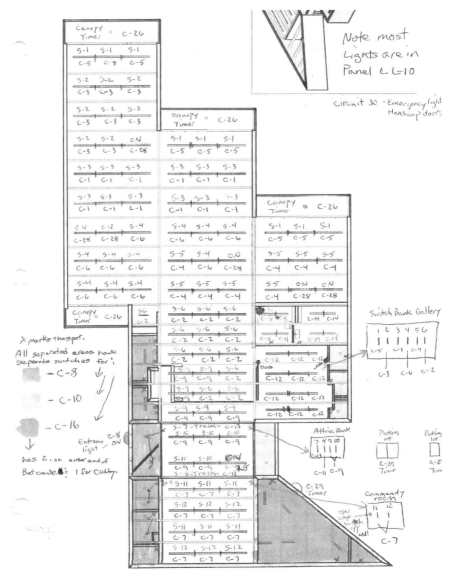

Figure 1.1. This map details both the circuits on which all of the museum's lighting are wired and the switches that control them. This makes it easy to determine which circuits to shut down when work must be done. The museum has a similar map for all of the outlets in the building, to make sure that individual circuits are not overloaded. (Courtesy of North Star Museum of Boy Scouting and Girl Scouting)

plowing your grounds as an in-kind donation; however, you will likely be low on the priority list as a nonpaying customer. A volunteer with a truck and plow blade can perform this work.

Volunteers maintain gardens at many museums. If the gardens at your institution are more decorative than an integral part of your interpretive program, there is no reason not to turn them over to garden clubs, master gardeners, or others with interest and ability. If your gardens are a critical part of the interpretation at your museum or site, then someone well versed in historical horticulture can provide a plan that others can carry out. In either case, you must be willing to provide your gardeners with the materials they need to carry out their tasks, like mulch, annuals, and tools. And if you have a garden, you must be willing to spend some money on watering. Nothing looks worse than an ill-kept garden with dying vegetation.

Both the Boy and Girl Scouts consider service to be an important part of their program, and you may be able to find troops willing to do some of your periodic maintenance (leaf raking or spring cleanup, for example) if you do some asking around. Other youth groups may be similarly available.

Periodic tasks will likely require professionals. If, for example, you have a considerable number of trees on your property, you should have an arborist take a look at them about every five years. Weakened and diseased trees pose a threat to property, visitors, and staff. Best to remove them before they fall down.

Preventative Maintenance

Like preventive conservation, preventive maintenance is key to a long and happy life in your building. Certain tasks, if carried out on a regular basis, will extend the life of the structure and building systems, as well as improve security and safety for staff and visitors.

Regular cleaning is one such task. A great example is vacuuming carpets and sweeping floors on a weekly basis (or daily, if you have very high visitation). Dirt tracked in on shoes and boots can be very damaging to carpet fibers, and will introduce more dust into your building. Hours of vacuuming and floor washing can be avoided by ensuring the cleanliness of the walks leading to your entry doors. Regularly vacuuming carpets (not historic carpets in a historic house museum, which are treated differently) lengthens their life and aids greatly in keeping down dust. Floor mats at all exterior doors are a relatively inexpensive investment to aid in keeping your building clean.

Dusting is another example of good preventative maintenance. Do not neglect high ledges, window frames, exhibit walls, or any other surface that can gather dust. Monthly, quarterly, or annual dusting of hard-to-reach places helps preserve your artifacts and enhances the appearance of your facility.

Photo 1.2. Well-maintained property is inviting to visitors and an important part of maintenance *inside* your buildings. Clean sidewalks (or, in this case, boardwalks) keep visitors from tracking dust, dirt, and other detritus into your building, saving you hours of sweeping, vacuuming, and mopping. (Photograph by Helen Alten for Northern States Conservation Center ©2004)

Many museums close for some time during the year. During this downtime, staff may clean exhibits. While staff supervised by conservators may clean the artifacts themselves, the exhibit furniture, cases, rails, and platforms should also be cleaned. This helps prevent the luring of pests into your building and gives your visitors the best impression of your commitment to preserving what you have. Safe cleaning materials for use in gallery and storage spaces should be identified by consulting conservators and scrupulously adhered to. The American Institute for Conservation of Historic and Artistic Works website has an extensive resource section that outlines these principles (see resource section at the end of this chapter).

All of the above procedures can be covered in a written housekeeping plan that contains the schedules, materials, and procedures in writing. For more information on creating a housekeeping plan, see the Minnesota Historical Society's *Housekeeping Handbook*, available online (see www.conservation-us.org). While written specifically for historic sites, it includes all the elements of a housekeeping plan you can create for your museum.

Changing Filters and Batteries

Depending on the environment surrounding your building, your HVAC system's filters may capture a great deal of dust, pollen, insects, and other detritus as the system brings in outside air and circulates it through your building. Just like at home, changing the filters on a regular basis (our HVAC contractor recommends monthly) ensures that your air-handling system functions efficiently and without damage. The facilities manager is in charge of seeing that this is done, and this work can be performed by anyone willing to become familiar with both the method of changing the filters and the safety precautions one must take when doing so.

Likewise, some tools and systems may require periodic battery changes to ensure that they operate when needed. While your smoke detectors or fire alarm system will be hardwired into your electrical system, many of these alarm panels have a backup battery to ensure that they will sound even in the event of a power failure. Consider other equipment that uses batteries, including data loggers, flashlights, and audiovisual equipment. Changing such batteries should be on the regular maintenance schedule.

Cyclical Maintenance

Roof Inspections

A periodic roof inspection helps ensure that your roof continues to do its job for you well, and you can get a heads-up if the roof shows signs of beginning to fail. A tight lid is critical to everything that happens beneath it.

Heating, Ventilating, and Air Conditioning Periodic Service

Your HVAC contractor will set up a regular schedule of service for your units. While you are responsible for changing filters or other basics that ensure your system runs at the peak efficiency that it is within your power to provide, it is also crucial for professionals to look over the system once or twice a year. Our units are serviced twice a year, usually at the change of seasons, when we switch from heating to air conditioning, and vice versa. This important inspection allows the technician to identify potential problems—scorch marks around a circuit, for example, that you probably would not catch. These inspections are covered in a yearly maintenance contract with your HVAC company.

Fire Inspections

You should expect a yearly inspection by your jurisdiction's fire marshal. It is this person's job to ensure that your building is safe for public gathering. Often, he or she will find problems that have otherwise gone overlooked (such as burned-out exit lights, uncovered junction boxes, or a lack of covers on outdoor electric sockets). Look at the fire marshal as a partner in your efforts to protect both your collection and your staff and visitors. This person has the power to compel you to do things you might not have had on your agenda, but in the end, it is for good reason and will enhance safety at your institution. At my museum, for example, fire marshals had not been around to inspect local businesses for a number of years. Our inspection was very cordial, and the violations that the fire marshal found were easily corrected the next day. However, when we received the correction notice, he had included one other thing we did not discuss—installing smoke detectors throughout the building. This work was on my mind, and we would have gotten to it eventually. Despite the unanticipated expense, our building is now safer for both the public and our collections. Do not be afraid to talk frankly with your fire inspector and to ask about potential surprises in a correction notice.

Fire Alarm and Security System Maintenance and Testing

This must be done yearly—without question. Aside from your HVAC system, your fire alarm system is the most important tool in keeping a safe building. You should have a contractor responsible for your system, and you should schedule yearly maintenance of the system, as well as monthly testing of the alarm keypad and panel. If you are fortunate enough to have a security system as well, this should be tested every year too. It is critical that these systems are operational at all times so that they can do their important jobs.

Integrated Pest Management

Pests only come into your institution when they are invited. Because much of what we might have in a museum has the potential to be a screaming invitation to pests of many kinds, we should make a commitment to reducing the number of additional invitations that we issue to these destructive critters.

Integrated pest management is a program of preventing pests from becoming a problem at your institution. It requires, first, that you inspect your building to locate evidence of current pest infestation. Then, it requires that you monitor these pests through the placement of traps around your facility. (IPM experts keep spreadsheets of the location of these traps and their weekly findings as a way of tracking the ebb and flow of infestations.) Once you know what kinds of pests you are dealing with, you begin to address the ways of keeping them out. The first step is blocking access to your facility by filling holes and cracks on the outside, clearing away landscape plants that attract museum pests, and installing sweeps on the bottoms of all doors so that they cannot simply walk in.

All organic material that comes into the museum should be inspected in an isolated place before it enters too far into your facility. Potential collections are generally inspected and often frozen (through a series of freeze-thaw cycles outlined at www.museumpests.net and at other conservation websites) to kill potential invaders. Staff members are generally prohibited from bringing personal plants into the building, and, as a rule, live plants should not be permitted. Food is limited to one area; trash bins with food in them are emptied daily, as are vacuum bags.

Pest management is one area of facility maintenance that requires a policy so that it can be shared with all users of the building—staff, board members, and outside groups. Dealing with incoming collections (I once trapped a shrew on a sticky trap after bringing in a plastic box of ceramic mugs that had been stored in a garage), storing reusable crates (particularly from traveling exhibits), and employee behavior with respect to bringing organic material into the museum from home or elsewhere all need to be addressed, and staff should be trained in not just the wherefores but also the whys of IPM. Adopting and sharing a formal IPM policy helps you educate anyone who uses the building as to why there are limits on organic material and ensures your collection is safe from creatures that would consume it.

Going Green

This area of facility maintenance has gotten much more talk than action. However, some aspects of sustainable building operations are worth considering as you operate your museum.

Consider your institutional values. As a museum of Boy and Girl Scouting, for example, my museum takes environmental responsibility very seriously. We know that burning fossil fuels to heat our building in winter and using electricity generated at outdated power plants to cool it in the summer do not add up to the most environmentally responsible way to go. If we are to be true to the values of the organizations whose work we are documenting, then we ought to be responsible about how we heat and cool our building, as well as how we manage our grounds.

History museums are in the forever business, after all, so take the time to look at the long-term benefits of green activities. At present, "going green" requires a significant upfront investment for any institution that retrofits its facility with more sustainable technology. However, in the long run, doing so is likely to be of enormous benefit to the bottom line, as well as the planet. Utility costs are generally the second-largest line item, following salaries, at any museum. If sinking a geothermal well or putting solar panels on the roof will cut the costs of heating and cooling the building in the long run, it should be considered. Grant funds may be available to assist with this type of investment in the future.

The area around your facility also provides opportunities for environmentally sound changes. Pavement in parking lots can be replaced with permeable surfaces to prevent runoff. These permeable surfaces have the added advantage, in cooler climes, of reducing the amount of plowing and snow-melting chemicals needed during the winter. To minimize runoff, use rain gardens. Cut the grass high and let it lie, compost clippings, and use strategic plantings to help keep your building cooler in the summer and warmer in the winter. By considering your institutional values, along with the short- and long-term costs and benefits of green building technology, you will have the tools to make decisions that make sense for your organization both in terms of pursuing your mission and ensuring your financial sustainability.

Funding Maintenance

Nowhere but in building operations can you be assured that you will have certain fixed expenses, month in and month out, year after year. You must have your HVAC system serviced. You must have your fire and burglar alarm systems tested each year. You must paint. You must clean. And at some point, roofs and HVAC systems must be replaced. The best way to ensure that these things get done, when necessary and without eating a hole in your operating budget, is to set up an endowment for maintenance or budget your surplus for future expenses. It can be difficult to find donors to support such work, but there are ways to sell it to potential donors. The donor who established our maintenance fund said to me, "You ignore the furnace for years because you think the money can be better spent on programs, and then it blows up!" Catastrophic failure of one of your building systems is going to cost you much more than if you replace aging and inefficient systems in due course.

The reason for doing regular and cyclical maintenance of our facilities, considering green technologies, writing policies and training staff in IPM, and setting up and following an operations manual under the guidance of a facilities manager is to make our institutions better, safer, and more operationally efficient. By doing this at the lowest cost possible, we are best able to pursue our mandate: to preserve permanently the materials that we have collected in order to tell their stories to future generations.

Safety and Security

Safety and security are of a piece, and they do not require lots of money or elaborate electronic equipment. Both can be achieved through low-cost, commonsense methods. Let us begin with the exterior of the building and work our way inside to the staff, visitors, and collections.

Your property should be well lit, especially at all entrances. This allows passing people (especially police) to see the exterior of your building at all times and easily determine if anyone suspicious is lurking someplace he or she ought not to be. Keeping shrubs and trees trimmed away from windows is also helpful. A burglar can easily hide in a shrub and enter your building through a window if no one can see him there. At a minimum, all doors and windows should be locked when the museum is not open.

Photo 1.3. The puddle of water underneath the water pipes is bad enough and should be discovered during a regular inspection of the facility. It is important that someone walk the grounds, around the exterior of the building, and around the inside of the building as frequently as you can manage. If left alone, this small leak could become a large flood. Even more distressing is the open cellar window. If no one goes down into this cellar for days, a thief could easily enter the facility. (Photograph by Helen Alten for Northern States Conservation Center ©2001)

A strongly enforced key program and policy is essential to good security. The master key is a sacred object. The head of security for 3M Corporation told me that there should be only one master key, and no one should carry it. The loss of a master key is catastrophic to your institution's security, requiring you to recall all distributed keys and rekey the building (which can be a very expensive proposition). All individuals granted the right to carry a key to your institution should be given the absolute minimum access needed to accomplish their tasks. Beyond access to the building, any other keys personnel need to carry out work inside should be available to them once they have entered. These keys should be kept in a locked and controlled key box and signed out when they are taken. As a matter of policy, keys to the collections storage areas should never be removed from the premises. This simple act of controlling your keys will make your institution much more secure.

If you have an electronic security system in addition to keys, you have some additional concerns. First, work with a security contractor with whom you feel comfortable. I suggest working with a local company. Although large, national companies will tell you that their call center is open 24/7 and your account is monitored at all times, a security company in your area knows immediately if a tornado has just blown through or a regionwide blackout has just occurred. Because their customer base is generally smaller than that of a nationwide company with a remote call center, local companies are much more likely to notice if something odd is going on with your account. For example, we had been using a large, national company for building security. For several nights running, I received 2 a.m. calls that our daily "line test" had failed. (The company tested our system so that it dialed in to them, as if an alarm had gone off.) It took three visits from a technician to diagnose the problem: Our system was programmed to dial a local number that was itself out of order! I cannot imagine that we were the only customers having such a problem, but with thousands of customers regionally and millions of customers nationally, how would the company notice? I prefer a monitoring service that does not have to ask me what kind of weather we had the previous night.

Interview your security company about how it deals with different types of alarms. Generally you have the option of customizing responses. For example, at my museum, any fire alarm at the museum requires the security company to directly dispatch the fire department. Burglar alarms, however, are first called in to the people on the call list. Recently, I received several calls at 3 or 4 a.m. about one particular motion detector that had gone off. On day two, I saw a mouse in the museum, and on night three, when I got the call, I was informed that mice do indeed set off the motion detector. Many police jurisdictions allow false alarms a couple of times a year and then charge a fee for responses after that number is exceeded; fortunately for us, we did not have to use up any of our freebies. If you have pests or anything else in the museum that is likely to set off a motion detector in the middle of the night, you might want to allow someone in authority to decide whether or not to dispatch police. (I must admit that while checking out the museum at 4 a.m. the first night, I did have my cell phone in hand.) Staff member safety should be balanced with risk of actual harm.

As with keys, only certain individuals should be given codes to disarm a fire or burglar alarm. Again, the number of people with this information should be kept to a minimum, and their access should be limited. Most electronic systems allow you to set a level of access, and most individuals should get the minimum necessary to carry out their work. Your security policy will dictate how often the alarm codes are changed. Alarm codes for each individual should be recorded on a spreadsheet and kept secure, and the alarm use in the building should be audited from time to time (does anyone who can disarm the security system have the opportunity to be in the building alone?). Your security contractor can provide you with alarm logs, and you can audit them on an irregular schedule just to see if anyone is coming or going when they ought not to be.

If you have had an electronic security system for a long time, it is possible that it operates through a phone line that is not protected outside the building. Today, all security systems will sound an alarm if the phone line is disabled. Several years ago at a rural historic site, thieves cut the phone line and spent several hours over a period of days going through the artifacts and packing what they intended to steal. They carried away some artifacts but left boxes of others to be taken at a later time. They obviously knew from surveillance of the site that no one was likely to come by, but they certainly risked having the security system sound an alarm if they cut the phone line. It did not. This is surely a discussion you should have with your security company, and check to see how the line is secured outside the building. You want to ensure that thieves cannot disable any of your building's systems by cutting wires outside the structure.

Your security policy will drive staffing of the museum, particularly during evenings, weekends, and holidays. Is staff allowed to work alone? On evenings and weekends, do people work in pairs? What kind of staffing is required for special events? Are specific tasks, like counting out a cash drawer, to be done in pairs, with each person witnessing the other? Does your security company have a panic button program? Museums in certain locations may wish to have a panic button near the main entrance for the protection of employees and visitors.

Security cameras are a welcome adjunct to a security program if you have areas of your gallery that staff cannot see during their normal work and you have particularly valuable material on exhibit. Their cost continues to come down, and if they are publicized and visible, they can have a deterrent effect upon potential thieves.

A less costly way to manage gallery security, however, is to implement a visitor-focused policy. Each person who enters the building should be greeted, their business with the museum should be determined, and they should be given any special instructions they will need for their visit. If your gallery space is small and a staff person at an entrance desk can see the entire space, then you can keep an eye on visitors. Be wary of distractions created by an accomplice (or just another innocent visitor). This is good justification for having staff work in pairs.

Another mistake that small museums often make is putting out display cases with easily defeated locks. Sometimes we get our cases from wherever we can—especially if they are free or inexpensive. Old store display cases can be opened easily, and a regular small lock can be picked in a trice. More than fifteen years ago, small museums across the Great Plains region were plagued with a series of thefts from their exhibits. The thieves often came into the museum during the lunch hour, when fewer people were around. Alone in a gallery with precious artifacts displayed in cases with bad locks, the thieves were in the cases and out of the museum in less than ten minutes. They stole valuable artifacts that were easily accessible. If you put artifacts on display, minimally secured or not secured at all in open displays, with the idea that visitors will never be in the galleries alone, perhaps you should rethink your strategy. Anything that you deem worth exhibiting is probably considered worth stealing by someone.

More insidious than the theft from an exhibit that is discovered immediately is the theft that is not discovered for some time. The sooner a theft is discovered, the more likely it is that the authorities will be able to recover the property. One way to ensure that thefts from an exhibit are discovered in a reasonable period is having a collections management policy that requires checklist inventories of exhibits on a periodic basis. If your exhibit space is small, you can do these daily or weekly. If your exhibit space is larger, you can do random spot checks. Any staff member can be trained to do this work.

And you need to think about staffing the museum during times when you might not be open to the public, but doors are open to let in people who might have other business with the institution. A contribution jar or other container near the entrance is an inviting target for thieves. Large bills should be removed from contribution containers every night and secured with other cash. Visitors should never be able to enter and leave the museum unseen.

Finally, there is always the possibility of a visitor threatening staff or other visitors. Any staff member on duty should have access to a telephone with local emergency numbers posted right next to it (including those for the gas and electric companies, the water utility, and your security company). Publications cited in the resource section have some excellent checklists for dealing with unruly or threatening members of the public (see Burke's *A Manual of Basic Museum Security* or Liston's *Museum Security and Protection*). The Department of Homeland Security has a very good publication on dealing with an "active shooter." (After the United States Holocaust Memorial Museum shooting in 2009, we are dealing with security threats that we could never have imagined twenty years ago.) The bottom line is that members of the museum staff have a responsibility to keep museum visitors, volunteers, and staff safe, without putting their own lives in jeopardy. This may mean herding visitors into a safe area that can be locked and calling the authorities.

Like most schools, museums should regularly schedule "lockdown" and fire drills. These allow staff to train in protecting visitors and responding automatically. In tornado country, a sheltered space within your institution (or on your grounds) should be identified, and you should train regularly on moving visitors to safe spaces. If you have a large property and many well-attended outdoor events, you should consider what you would do in the event of a sudden storm.

It is critical that all museums develop an emergency response plan to cover many of the events described above. Each event will dictate a different kind of response, and staff should be regularly trained in carrying out these emergency responses. This plan is separate and apart from the disaster plan, although they should work in conjunction with each other. The emergency response plan deals primarily with the staff and visitors to your institution and is designed to ensure that all are safe, no matter what the disaster or emergency. There are many excellent sources of examples of emergency response plans, most notably from the Federal Emergency Management Administration (FEMA).

Risk Assessments

When you look around your facility, you are very unlikely to see everything that someone trained in risk management might see. Perhaps you are blocking a fire exit because that seems to be the only place where you can put a display case, large piece of equipment, or artifact. You may not realize that running multiple extension cords across the floor poses a tripping hazard or that piling combustibles (as fire marshals and risk managers call flammable material) near a water heater is dangerous. You may figure that putting out a "Wet Floor" sign when washing the bathroom floor in the morning will not be necessary because no one will be in the building. Bringing in a professional with risk management expertise can be an eye-opening experience for you.

These types of assessments need not cost anything. Insurance companies are often pleased to help you figure out what you can do better to minimize risk to staff and visitors (or your building). The regional conservation centers across the United States have staff experienced in disaster response who are very knowledgeable about minimizing and mitigating risk. Don't forget that your local police and fire departments have expertise and can help you. In fact, you should plan on inviting all local police officers and firefighters to your museum on a regular basis, just so that they know who you are, what you are doing, what you have in your building, and where it is located. Police officers and firefighters are curious about what goes on behind your doors, and specific knowledge of what you have and how you value it can help them respond better to your institution.

Once you have walked through your building with a risk manager, you will never look at the place in the same way again. When you become aware of the potential hazards, you have an opportunity to make your staff, visitors, and collection safer. The good news is that many of the fixes will cost very little. Moving furniture and equipment and being more mindful of potential dangers will go a long way toward protecting everything that is important to you.

Collections Management as a Security Tool

Collections management is tackled in detail in chapter 3 of Book 6, but from a security standpoint, collections management procedures cannot be minimized as an important tool in keeping your institution secure. All collection storage areas should have visitor logs that must be signed each time someone enters and exits the space. This should hold for staff as well as visitors. In addition to the exhibition inventories mentioned above, regular inventories of the collection will help you keep track of what you have and make you aware either of truly missing items or failures in procedure that send artifacts into limbo. While full-collection inventories require a lot of man-hours (and so may take time away from other projects), they should be scheduled on a regular basis (perhaps every three to five years). Spot checks of both records and artifacts should be carried out at least quarterly (take ten records and find the corresponding artifacts, then pick ten artifacts off the shelf and find the corresponding records).

Movement of artifacts around the museum (especially taking an artifact off exhibition) should always be tracked and documented. Nothing should be removed from an exhibition unless it is replaced with an "out" card, signed by staff members with the appropriate authority, and the location of the artifact should be changed in the written or computerized record as it moves. A similar card should be used in collections storage when an item goes on display.

These techniques cost nothing except time and planning. Enshrine them in policy, lay them out in procedures, and ensure that everyone follows them every time. If you are the director, curator, or board president, be sure to set a good example by never taking shortcuts.

Disaster Planning

A written disaster plan is a key component of safety and security for the institution and one of the cornerstones of museum operations. Everything that you do in managing your facility should be geared toward preventing disaster at the institutional level. But we all know that no matter how prepared we might be for a disaster in our facility, sometimes events and circumstances are just beyond our control. That said, a well-written, well-thought-out, up-to-date disaster plan is an invaluable aid in protecting your institution in the event of any kind of disaster. Given the amount of written material on disaster planning and the number of workshops on the topic, it is astounding that more institutions do not have an up-to-date, complete disaster plan on their shelves. Make sure that it becomes an institutional priority if you do not already have one.

The wrong time to begin thinking about a disaster plan is when one is unfolding before your eyes. When a disaster occurs, it is an emotional blow to the staff that can short-circuit rational thought. If, however, you have a disaster plan ready—one developed when all was calm and the staff was thinking clearly—you will have someplace to look for guidance, and it will tell you what to do! When rational thought has temporarily fled, there is nothing like having checklists, call lists, and instructions to keep you moving productively.

The preparation of an institutional disaster plan can be enormously beneficial to you. It forces you to think hard about what can or might happen, what kind of response you will need to make, what it will cost, what insurance coverage you will need to recover, who will help you, and who will be in charge. It forces you to think hard about postdisaster safety and to clarify your collections recovery priorities.

Photo 1.4. How well would you function if this was your museum? A disaster plan is the only thing that will tell you what to do next. (Photograph by Helen Alten for Northern States Conservation Center ©1999)

Photo 1.5. No one alive in Faribault, Minnesota, could remember the confluence of the Straight and Canon Rivers ever being as high as it is in this photograph, after a series of hard rains in September 2010. The executive director of the Rice County Historical Society, Susan Garwood, said, "We're definitely changing our approach to flood preparation." The two rivers join five hundred yards from the museum's front door, and they escaped water in the building by only three vertical inches. (Courtesy of Rice County Historical Society)

Perhaps best of all, good disaster planning will force you to do those things you know you should do but have not—like duplicate (or back up) your records and store them off-site. Or get to know your neighboring historical organizations—perhaps to the point where you can organize a disaster response co-op. (The basic supplies to respond to a disaster at a museum are remarkably similar and generally must be stored off-site. Perhaps you and your neighboring museums can share the costs and store supplies for other institutions nearby.) The resource section at the end of this chapter contains some excellent references on disaster planning, and regional conservation labs regularly run workshops. Check online for the next one near you.

Use national events as springboards for your disaster and emergency planning. MayDay, sponsored by Heritage Preservation and other members of the Heritage Emergency National Task Force, provides an annual reminder to work for disaster preparedness. You can use this day to update disaster plans, hold training events for your staff, and meet with local emergency responders to ensure the future safety of your collections. October is Fire Prevention Month and, as such, is a good time to conduct an annual fire drill (and, if you live in a tornado-prone area, a tornado drill as well). More frequent drills are helpful for staff to review their responsibilities for visitors and collections so they know what to do in the event of the real thing.

Accident or Incident Reporting

In the event of an injury to a visitor, an incident report form should be filled out. This provides you with the information you will need to follow up with the injured person and notify your liability insurance carrier. A "First Report of Injury" form should be filled out every time someone is injured on the job (including volunteers). In the event of injury to paid staff on the job, workers' compensation insurance has its own reporting forms, which can usually be obtained from the department in your state that administers workers' compensation.

Insurance

Insurance is one of those things that we do not like to think about. Insurance agents use language that the layperson finds difficult to understand, and the product seems very expensive for something we hope never to use. Yet state and federal laws mandate some types of insurance for all businesses (and yes, we are businesses), and common sense dictates that we should have other types of insurance. Insurers will recommend that you read your policy when you get it; you should never be reading your insurance policy while the sprinklers are going off or while you are standing in your parking lot, watching the fire department pour millions of gallons of water onto your building. Insurance agents like to talk about their product, and you would do well to get to know your agent. If you live in a small community, you and your agent may educate each other about when you need specialized insurance (like fine arts insurance for a loan or for your collections). Get to know your agent, and get him or her on your side.

Insurance protects your institution from loss in the event of unforeseen circumstances. If your treasurer embezzles tens of thousands of dollars from your museum, directors and officers insurance might be able to help you. If a tree falls on your building and punches a hole in the roof, your building property insurance will help. If a kid falls in your parking lot and injures his head, your liability insurance will help. And if a valuable loaned object is stolen from your gallery, fine arts insurance could come to your rescue. As a director or board member, it is your responsibility to ensure that the institution does not suffer financial reverses. Insurance is an investment you make to guarantee that.

Building and Contents Insurance

Insuring your building against loss is a fairly straightforward exercise. The underwriters know the general value of your building and property and will set a figure. If you have made improvements to the structure, you should make sure your insurer recalculates the insurance value of the building. You will not really be insuring the building for anything different than you would for any other business structure. But if you make changes in the building that might lower the insurance company's burden (like installing smoke detectors), let your agent know—it might lower your premium. In our case, we significantly increased the probability that a fire would be detected sooner and, since the fire department is a block and a half from our building, be put out sooner, thereby sparing the structure. We saved about 10 percent on our insurance premiums after this work was done.

Make sure that you set policy limits and deductibles carefully. While a higher deductible will save you on premiums, if you do not have enough cash reserves to pay up to the deductible out of pocket, you should rethink. Likewise, a policy limit has to be high enough to allow you to recover and return to normal operations in the event of a disaster or other claimable event. Make sure that the limit is sufficient.

Insuring contents is another matter. Desks, computers, chairs, tables, and the like are assets of your nonprofit corporation and should be inventoried yearly. Insuring the contents (excluding collections) of your building is important. Insurance agents will generally come up with a catchall value that will allow you to replace some of the contents of the museum, but if you have purchased or added new equipment, it is worth having a conversation with your insurer to increase the value of your noncollection contents. In the event of a disaster, you will need desks, chairs, and computers to get your operations up and running again.

Insuring your collections against loss is only related to museum operations through your disaster plan. Small museum directors are sometimes encouraged by their boards to insure the entire collection against loss. This is folly. The value of historical artifacts varies with market conditions. Any insurance value set by an institution for an object in its collection must be supported by research into current market values and the sale prices for similar items. Updating the insurance values of your entire collection would take hundreds of hours to complete—and you would have to do it every year. A wiser course is to identify valuable key artifacts in your collection, the loss of which would negatively impact your program or the partial loss of which would cost thousands of dollars in treatments by a conservator. If you have such artifacts, you can schedule them on your insurance policy. Then, you should take a look at your disaster plan and assess how much it would cost you to treat all or part of your collection in the event of a building-wide disaster, like a fire or flood. This amount should be added to your policy as disaster recovery funds for unscheduled property in your custody. The chances of a total loss are generally remote. The chance that you might suffer loss of or damage to one of your key artifacts is greater. Therefore, secure insurance coverage for that which seems most likely.

Liability Insurance

Liability coverage is one of the most important types of insurance you will have for your organization. This is the kind of insurance that minimizes your institution's financial loss if it is responsible (or even if it is not responsible) for someone else's loss while on your property. I ask kids on skateboards to leave our property all the time because their activity poses an unacceptable risk for us. They are not participating in our program and are only using our parking lot to practice jumps and other dangerous maneuvers. They do not have safety equipment or supervision. If they got hurt (I am thinking head injury), their parents would be within their rights to come after us (whether a court would hold us liable is another matter). I tell the kids this, and they insist that their parents would do no such thing. I know better.

But even if you take all the recommendations of this chapter and fully implement them to make your institution as safe and risk-free as possible, someone might still be injured. An elderly woman could fall, a kid could tip over in a chair, one of your carefully hung signs could fall on a visitor's head, or you could have an institution-wide disaster with injuries. As with building and contents insurance, set limits and deductibles on your liability insurance carefully. Make sure that if more than one person is injured at a time, all are covered. Make sure that you have the cash reserves to cover your deductible and that a judgment against you would not bankrupt your organization. Taking the safety and security of staff and visitors seriously, and being able to prove that you are doing so, will help mitigate any damage judgment.

Use your insurance agent as a resource to help you determine what you need. When you first sign up for insurance, he or she will likely hand you a boilerplate business policy. You need to read it, pay attention to the deductibles and policy limits, and talk with the board about what levels of insurance you need and what you can afford. While any lender will require building insurance, no one will ask to see your liability insurance policy. But woes betide you if you do not have one.

It can be a useful exercise for the institution's management to review the overall risk annually or every few years. Include the director, the facilities manager, the facilities committee, and possibly the executive committee. The agenda should include review of any incidents during the previous year, the levels of coverage, and any building upgrades and could conclude with a walk-through of the facility to determine if anything needs to be changed. This hour-long meeting could save you money, might prevent injury, and will make your facility a better and safer place to visit.

Workers' Compensation Insurance

The state and federal governments require you to have workers' compensation insurance if you employ staff. There are severe fines and penalties if you do not have this type of insurance, so make sure your agent handles this for you too. (You can often save on premiums if you buy more than one type of insurance from the same carrier.) Workers' compensation insurance is based on the relative dangerousness of the occupations at your museum. The cost for the director's insurance is going to be many times lower than that for a maintenance person's, for example, because the director does nothing more dangerous than sit at a desk, walk and talk at the same time, or drive a car. Rates drop over the years if there are no claims, so while the cost may seem high initially, it will drop if you run a safe workplace. State and federal laws also require you to post information about where employees can report injuries and that you have "First Report of Injury" forms available for employees to fill out if they are injured.

Directors and Officers Insurance

D&O insurance protects the board and management from personal liability in the event of loss through fraud or theft or in the event of an institutional bankruptcy with significant debt. Without it, the board and top management could be held personally liable for the debts of the corporation. It is difficult to attract top-flight talent to a board without it, and smart candidates will ask about it before seriously considering joining your board.

Insurance is a necessity. It protects the institution from loss, provides a means to compensate injured parties, and creates an incentive to run a safe, secure organization. Insurance companies want to help you reduce your risk because they do not want to pay claims, just as you do not want to have to make them. But when insurance is needed, nothing else can take its place.

Building Rental or Use

Building rental or use can be a wonderful way to extend your reach to the broader community. If you have a pretty setting and the space, hosting rental events can provide a significant source of income and allow you to support your mission-related expenses. Building use by individuals who are carrying out events that align with your mission are different animals.

Table 1.1. Types of Insurance

Types of Insurance	Value to Institution
Building and Contents	Ordinarily part of a business owner's policy, this insures against loss of the structure due to fire, tornado, explosion, or other natural or man-made disasters. In the museum context, "contents" refers strictly to tables, chairs, computers, and other tools of your business—but not the collection.
Collections/Disaster Recovery	If you have valuable, important, or fragile artifacts, you can set a value for them and include them as part of your collections insurance. Otherwise, you will use a figure generated by your disaster planning to determine how much you would need to recover damaged items from your collection from a partial disaster. This would be used to obtain recovery supplies and helpers, cover undamaged collections, and the like.
Liability	This insurance is absolutely necessary and will protect the institution in the event that a visitor is injured on your premises, either through negligence or not. This includes kids skateboarding in your parking lot without your permission or a visitor on a guided tour getting clobbered by a falling tree branch.
Workers' Compensation	This insurance is required by state law, and you cannot go without it. It covers employees if injured in the line of duty, and can cover volunteers as well. Requires a "First Report of Injury" form to be immediately filed when there is an injury on the job.
Directors and Officers	This protects all board members and senior staff from liability in the event of internal theft or embezzlement, or action arising out of the dissolution of the corporation.
Fine Arts	This insurance is generally necessary when you are borrowing an item from another museum's collection or taking in a traveling exhibition. It covers the art and artifacts from the time they leave the wall at the originating institution until they are returned to the wall there (thus the appellation, "Wall to Wall" coverage).
Motor Vehicle	This insurance is for museum vehicles.

Rental Events

The board and staff should carefully weigh the costs and benefits of allowing rental events that do not relate to a museum's mission. If brides wish to marry at the museum because it is pretty or has a wonderful event space, the fees paid count as unrelated business income (UBIT) and are subject to taxes. However, there is no shame in paying UBIT—if you end up netting more than your costs, it helps your bottom line. If these rental events allow you to do more because you have more money, you may decide that they are worth it.

Rental events are not just an income stream. Wear and tear on museums and historic sites from rental events is real. Guests who have had too much to drink sometimes abuse the property, and you will likely need increased liability insurance. If your site is popular, you can expect high demand. Will you be able to handle logistics, meeting with potential renters, staffing the event, managing billing and payment, following up if something happens, and other issues that are likely to arise when renting to outsiders?

If you decide that the benefits of income and increased community use of the building and grounds outweigh the costs of administering the rental program, then establish a carefully considered policy and use a rental agreement (see textbox 1.2 for questions to consider). Check out the policies and agreements of museums in your region to see what others require and what fee ranges are common. You might want to ask a lawyer to review your policy and agreement and to advise you on any disclaimers of liability that you might want to include.

Keep clear financial records for rental events and expect to pay taxes on them. If they are well managed, they can be a very good way to enhance your program by providing significant income with which to do your work.

Mission-Related Building Use

But what about building use by groups that align with your mission? Is it fair and wise to charge them fees to use your space? Mission-aligned building use by outside organizations can be a way of extending your work and mission beyond what you could ordinarily do with only your institution's resources. If you have a fee schedule for use of the building, you might wish to provide a significant discount to groups that use your building for mission-related activities.

For example, as a museum of Boy and Girl Scouting, my institution discounts use by Scout units or parents of Scouts who might wish to hold a Scouting event at the museum. We look at this as additional programming for us. In fact, if a Scout group wishes to use the museum for something that truly is program related (like an event for younger Girl Scouts, led by older girls as part of an advancement project), then the building use fee is waived entirely because we count the group's event as part of our program. When you have a small staff, this is an ideal way to increase the amount of programming that you do.

An institutional policy on mission-aligned building use by outside organizations helps you extend your reach. Our policy grants the director broad discretion in deciding how to consider and charge for these types of events, requiring only that the director report to the board the number of times that the waiver is granted. And because these events are mission related, the fees paid by the outside organizations are not taxable (and are tracked separately from rental income).

POLICY CONSIDERATIONS FOR RENTAL EVENTS

These are some of the things that you need to put into your policy regarding rental events at your institution:

- What kind of staffing will you require to manage such events?
- Who pays for staffing? Is it a separate charge to the renter, or is it included in the fee?
- Will you have a staff member whose job it is to run these events?
- How is the fee schedule structured? Is there an all-encompassing flat rate or is the service à la carte?
- When is your site available for rental? What hours is the facility available?
- Where can the event take place? Which parts of the property are open for rental and which are off-limits?
- How do you manage parking, keep people out of places where they are not supposed to be, and protect furniture and artifacts?
- How do you convey ground rules to guests?
- Do you have a list of approved caterers (people who know their way around your place and respect the property), or will you work with whomever the renter chooses?
- If the guests will be in a historic site, are there limits on types of food or beverages? (The State Department Diplomatic Reception Rooms in Washington, DC, have an extensive list of food and drink that are not allowed at parties in these spaces because of the historic furnishings and fixtures—for example, no red wine.)
- Who is responsible for setup and cleanup?
- Will you require a damage or other type of deposit?
- What is your cancellation and refund policy?

The policy related to these kinds of events is not terribly extensive:

- Who makes decisions about fees? Can you offer guidelines for fair application?
- Who sets up and cleans up?
- What kind of staffing is required?
- How do you convey ground rules to the users?

Conclusion

The purpose of a good museum operations program is to carry out your mission in a safe and secure place while simultaneously minimizing the risk to your staff, visitors, and collections. Effective operations provide a welcoming first impression to the public, a safe workplace for staff, a secure place to store and exhibit your artifacts, and a useful space in which to pursue your mission.

Properly managing your facility, security, and risk allows you the freedom to concentrate on what is important—serving the public and teaching the lessons that are yours to teach. In the meantime, you will know that you have done all you can to protect the resources with which you have been entrusted, and in the event of a calamity that no one could have foreseen, you will be ready and protected.

Resources

Facility

American Association of Museums Registrar's Committee. *General Facility Report.* 2nd ed. Washington, DC: AAM, 2008.

Brophy, Sara S., and Elizabeth Wylie. *The Green Museum: A Primer on Environmental Practice.* Lanham, MD: AltaMira Press, 2008.

Butcher-Younghans, Sherry, and Gretchen E. Anderson. *A Holistic Approach to Museum Pest Management.* American Association for State and Local History Technical Leaflet 191. Nashville, TN: AASLH, 1990.

Genoways, Hugh H., and Lynne M. Ireland. *Museum Administration: An Introduction.* Lanham, MD: AltaMira Press, 2003.

Harmon, James. *Integrated Pest Management in Museum, Library, and Archival Facilities: A Step by Step Approach for the Design, Development, Implementation, and Maintenance of an Integrated Pest Management Program.* Indianapolis: Harmon Preservation Pest Management, 1993.

Herman, Melanie L., George L. Head, Peggy M. Jackson, and Toni E. Fogarty. *Managing Risk in Nonprofit Organizations: A Comprehensive Guide.* Hoboken, NJ: John Wiley & Sons, 2003.

Integrated Pest Management Working Group. *Museum Pests.* www.museumpests.net (accessed May 15, 2011). (For information on freezing or low temperatures, see the "Low Temperature Treatment of Infested Cultural Materials" article under "Solutions Fact Sheets.")

Layne, Stevan P. *Cultural Property Protection Manual.* Denver, CO: Layne Consultants International, 2002.

Merritt, Elizabeth E. *Covering Your Assets: Facilities and Risk Management in Museums.* Washington, DC: American Association of Museums, 2005.

Minnesota Historical Society. *Historic Housekeeping Manual.* St. Paul, MN: Minnesota Historical Society, June 2000. Available for download at www.mnhs.org/preserve/conservation/reports/manual-0102.pdf.

Safety and Security

Adams-Graf, Diane, and Claudia J. Nicholson. "Thinking Ahead about Museum Security: An Ounce of Prevention Is Worth a Pound of Cure," *Tech Talk* (March 2000), www.mnhs.org/about/publications/techtalk/TechTalkMarch2000.pdf.

Architects Security Group. "Articles and Downloads." Architects Security Group. www.architectssecuritygroup.com/Consulting/Articles_and_Downloads.html (accessed May 15, 2011).

Burke, Robert B., and Sam Adeloye. *A Manual of Basic Museum Security.* Lanham, MD: University Press of America, 1989.

Department of Homeland Security. *Active Shooter: How to Respond.* Washington, DC: Department of Homeland Security, 2008. Available at www.dhs.gov/xlibrary/assets/active_shooter_booklet.pdf (accessed December 2, 2009).

Liston, David, ed. *Museum Security and Protection: A Handbook for Cultural Heritage Institutions.* London: Routledge/International Committee on Museum Security, 1993.

National Fire Protection Association. *NFPA 909: Standard for the Protection of Cultural Resources Including Museums, Libraries, Places of Worship, and Historic Properties.* Quincy, MA: NFPA, n.d.

———. *NFPA 914: Recommended Practice for Fire Protection in Historic Structures.* Quincy, MA: NFPA, n.d.

Disaster Planning

Dorge, Valerie, and Sharon L. Jones. *Building an Emergency Plan: A Guide for Museums and Other Cultural Institutions.* Los Angeles: Getty Conservation Institute, 1999.

Heritage Preservation. *Field Guide to Emergency Response.* Washington, DC: Heritage Preservation, 2006.

Iowa Cooperative Preservation Consortium. *Flood Recovery Booklet.* Iowa City: Iowa Cooperative Preservation Consortium, 1994.

Lord, Allyn, Carolyn Renol, and Marie Demeroukas. *Steal This Handbook! A Template for Creating a Museum's Emergency Preparedness Plan.* Columbia, SC: Southeastern Registrars Association, 1994.

National Fire Protection Association. *NFPA 909: Protection of Cultural Resources.* Quincy, MA: NFPA, 2009.

National Task Force on Emergency Response. *Emergency Response and Salvage Wheel.* Washington, DC: Heritage Preservation, 1997.

New York University Libraries Preservation Committee. *Disaster Plan Workbook.* New York: New York University Libraries, n.d. Available at http://library.nyu.edu/preservation/disaster/ch4.htm (accessed May 15, 2011).

Northeast Document Conservation Center and Massachusetts Board of Library Commissioners. "dPlan: The Online Disaster-Planning Tool for Cultural and Civic Institutions." dPlan. www.dplan.org (accessed February 11, 2011).

O'Connell, Mildred. "Disaster Planning: Writing and Implementing Plans for Collections-Holding Institutions." *Technology and Conservation* (Summer 1983): 18–24.

Reilly, Julie A. *Are You Prepared?* Omaha: Nebraska State Historical Society, 1997.

Trinkley, Michael. *Can You Stand the Heat? A Fire Safety Primer for Libraries, Archives and Museums.* Atlanta, GA: Southeastern Library Network, 1993.

Insurance

Flitner, Arthur. "An Insurance Primer for the Local Historical Organization." American Association for State and Local History Technical Leaflet 147. Nashville, TN: AASLH, 1983.

McGiffin, Gail E. "Sharing the Risk." *History News* 48, no. 1 (January–February 1993): 16–19.

Pontillo, Mary. *Covering Risk from Every Angle: Museum Insurance Handbook.* New York: DeWitt Stern Group, 2009. Available at www.dewittstern.com/docs/museum_insurance_guide_2009.pdf (accessed February 11, 2011).

Smith, Scott. "Insurance Planning." *History News* 48, no. 1 (January–February 1993): 18–19, 37.

Building Rental or Use

MacCarthy, Catherine, Caroline Cotgrove, Fiona Macalister, and Nettie Cook. "Events: Planning and Protection." In *Manual of Housekeeping: The Care of Collections in Historic Houses Open to the Public*, edited by National Trust, 722–33. London: National Trust, 2006.

HUMAN RESOURCES ADMINISTRATION: BUILDING AN EFFECTIVE TEAM

Patricia Anne Murphy

Effective human resource administration is crucial to the success of any small museum, be it an all-volunteer group or a museum where volunteers work together with one or more paid employees. This chapter provides strategies, practical suggestions, and ideas to help small museum personnel deal with human resources administration proactively, effectively, and efficiently. While human resources administration may sound like a very mundane and tedious subject, becoming effective in administering the people in your museum is key to your entire organization's success. Developing and implementing all the pesky policies and procedures to effectively manage human resources is essential to having a solid foundation for all you plan to achieve. This also helps everyone associated with your organization to understand their roles and responsibilities and how to function effectively as a team. In addition to the important subject of building an effective team, topics covered in this chapter include crafting a strong personnel manual of policies and procedures, developing job descriptions, working with volunteers who perform key staff functions, finding and hiring the most qualified person for the job, tackling evaluation of employees and using the process as a tool for performance improvement, addressing performance issues, fostering professional growth and skill development, and, last but not least, using standards, best practices, and other great resources that will help your museum succeed.

Teamwork: Bringing Staff (and Volunteers) Together

Building an effective team is essential to every small museum's success. Developing an effective human resources administrative strategy with a clear delineation of roles and responsibilities can help immensely in creating a team atmosphere because it gets and keeps everyone on the same page and working together collaboratively to accomplish the organization's mission. For example, volunteers who do a specific task at your museum regularly, such as typing spine labels for books in the library or posting event flyers in locations around town, will often find their sometimes rather mundane assignments much more meaningful if they feel part of a team. It also helps when they have a better understanding of the big picture and how what they are doing fits within the overall goals of moving the organization forward. Posting the organization's mission in a prominent location where staff and volunteers see it regularly is another simple way of reminding them of the bigger purpose of their work.

Many small museums are founded by an energetic and passionate individual or group of individuals with a common goal. As the institution evolves and the people involved in it change over time, it can become harder and harder to keep people working together toward a common goal or mission. The executive director must build on the successes of the founders but also move the museum forward.

Above all, if you are the museum director, remember that you are a facilitator and coordinator and that "it is not about you." Convey your passion for the mission of the organization. Give credit to the board, the staff, the volunteers, and your funders, and convey the message that "we" (not "I") are doing this together wherever possible.

Give Thanks Profusely

One of the most crucial ways to help people feel that they are part of the team is to devise strategies to effectively thank and salute those who help your museum in any way. Saying thank you often and creatively in person, by phone, through e-mail, or in your publications is one of the most important ways to ensure your success. Little gestures of kindness can go a long way toward motivating your team. Remember—it is not about you. Banish the word "I" from your vocabulary. Give your team the credit they deserve for all that you achieve together!

Saying thank you can also be a group team-building activity. Have the staff spend fifteen minutes at a staff meeting writing personal thank-you notes to people who helped at a recent event. Or, at the end of a board meeting, ask the board to write personal thank-yous on annual fund thank-you letters to people they know. Or nominate a volunteer for a statewide award. Get others on your team to write letters of support. Pack up a carload of people to attend and applaud. Bring your cameras and make sure to send copies of photos to all who participated as well as to the media. People who feel their efforts are genuinely appreciated are more apt to want to continue to help and to offer their financial support.

Showcase what has been accomplished (or ten great things that have been done that year) in an upbeat presentation at your annual membership meeting or holiday staff-volunteer gathering. This can help generate enthusiasm, encourage participation by new volunteers, and build team spirit for working together to accomplish your mission.

Photo 2.1. Nominating individuals and projects for awards and celebrating your successes helps to build a strong team. Several Oberlin Heritage Center board members, officers, past presidents, volunteers, and staff members are pictured here at the Ohio Association of Historical Societies and Museums annual meeting awards ceremony at the Ohio Historical Society on October 8, 2005. (Courtesy of Oberlin Heritage Center)

Photo 2.2. Oberlin Heritage Center key volunteers and staff members enjoy an annual holiday brunch. A presentation at the event showcases all they have accomplished in the previous year. Photographs are sent to everyone who attended as an extra thank-you, which makes everyone feel appreciated and part of the team. (Courtesy of Oberlin Heritage Center)

CHAPTER TWO

The Power of a Birthday Card

Another way to make your board, staff, and volunteers feel special and part of your team is by putting someone in charge of birthday cards. When people first become associated with your museum, ask for their birth date and month (not year, unless they volunteer it). Use this to create a chronological list of birth dates. Put someone with nice handwriting and access to your address list in charge of birthdays. By the fifteenth of each month (or other set date), this person should prepare a birthday card for everyone on the list and ask others to sign it or write a note. Bringing that month's cards to the board members and getting board members to write notes is especially effective, even if it adds a few minutes to the board meeting. Then, by the first of the month, put all the cards in order by date, and remember to send them out a few days before each person's birthday. Your team members will be all smiles. As an extra special touch, include an insert about what happened that day in history or include a photo of the team member taken at one of your events or at work in your museum. Or have a computer-savvy volunteer design a birthday card tailored to that team member for an especially big birthday. Bringing in goodies for a staff-volunteer gathering on or near a birthday is of course another effective way to shine the light on a valued team member.

Spread Good Will and Good News

With many volunteers, staff, and interns working at your museum during varying and occasional hours, a centrally located bulletin board in a behind-the-scenes location that they visit regularly, such as the break or coat room, can help keep people on the same page. This is especially recommended if not everyone uses e-mail to read your members' or volunteers' e-newsletter. Post flyers for upcoming events. Show off the great visitor feedback cards you have received recently. Tack up a postcard from Tom's trip to Tahiti. Showcase Sally's son's graduation picture. Add a photo of everyone who attended your holiday volunteer party. Warn people about ice on the walks. Show off an article about a recent award your organization won. Invite team members to a coffee break. Post a list of upcoming meetings, tours, and events and show who is going to be working which events and where additional volunteers are needed. The bulletin board is also a great place to post information about other community events. And keep it up to date so there is always a reason to read it.

Help Everyone Know Who's Who

Provide inexpensive name tags for each person who works at your site and ask that everyone wear them. You can make your own on the computer if you purchase vinyl, magnet-backed name-badge holders or lanyard-style badge holders. Use a large font size so that tags can be read from a few feet away. Your workers then are readily identifiable to visitors and to one another and can help to serve as on-site greeters and security detail. Volunteers who make deliveries or do other errands around town should also be encouraged to wear their name tags. If your budget permits, provide T-shirts, hats, or jackets with your logo on them to wear for a special event or whenever they wish.

Just the Facts

Develop a one-page fact sheet about your museum as a ready reference document that gives all the basic facts. It will be useful for orienting newcomers to your team and assures that team members always have the basic facts at their disposal, ready to share with others. This quick reference helps everyone feel confident and competent in representing the organization. Make it double sided if you need more room. This can be produced as a Word document on your computer so that it can be readily updated. It should include

- your logo (if you have one) or a photo of your museum;
- your mission;
- the history of the museum;
- a description of your board and a list of your board officers;
- a description of your facility;
- a description of your programs;
- a list of hours that you are open;
- a list of your publications;
- a list of awards and accomplishments;
- a description of your membership program;
- information about how people can contribute or volunteer;
- a list of key staff members and volunteers and their job titles;
- contact information, including mailing address, phone, website, and e-mail.

An example can be found on the Oberlin Heritage Center's website (www. oberlinheritage.org) by searching for "fact sheet."

The fact sheet can also be a valuable compilation of basic facts to go to when you are preparing a grant proposal or developing what professional fundraisers term a "case statement" to demonstrate to potential donors that they should fund your organization or its special project. Use it also to develop your "elevator speech" of the essentials of what your organization is about and why it is important, presented in the time it takes to ride the elevator. Your fact sheet can be given to prospective funders and members and included in a media packet you prepare for reporters or travel writers who may show up at your door unannounced. A simple pocket folder with your logo sticker on the cover works well for this purpose.[1]

Personnel Manual

A personnel manual outlines all the information and guidelines that employees need to do their jobs. It is an important tool to help employees become effective workers and community ambassadors for your museum. In thinking about preparing a personnel manual, it may be helpful to think about all the things you know now that you wish you had known when you first became affiliated with your museum, whether as a paid or volunteer staff member or a board member.

Have an attorney review your draft personnel manual and all draft personnel policies before they are enacted by the board of directors to ensure that you are in compliance with applicable local, state, and federal employment law. This can help prevent problems down the road.

Employees typically receive the personnel manual containing all personnel policies when they are hired, as part of an employee orientation process. The personnel manual can be easily adapted to serve as a volunteer manual. Please note that those items in the list below indicated by an asterisk would often appear in adapted form in a volunteer orientation manual. A typical personnel manual will often include the following sections:

- A letter of welcome from the executive director and board president.*
- Your mission statement, vision statement, and core values.*
- A brief summary of the history of the organization.*
- Employment and hiring procedures, including an Equal Employment Opportunity/nondiscrimination statement and policy and definition of exempt (salaried) and nonexempt (hourly) staff classifications.
- Your employee performance evaluation procedure.
- Professional development opportunities.
- Employee benefits (health insurance, workers' compensation, state unemployment insurance, retirement plan, and any nonmonetary incentives such as flexible scheduling, staff discount in the museum store, etc.).
- Paid time off (vacation, holidays, and sick time).
- Unpaid time off and leaves of absence (medical leave, military leave).
- Work hours and pay periods.
- Health and safety in the workplace (drug-free workplace, smoking policy, etc.).*

- Work practices and expectations (including use of facilities, property, and equipment; dress code; expectations regarding wearing name tags; expense reimbursement; parking requirements; issuance of keys, etc.).*
- Communication and confidentiality (including speaking to the media, not allowing soliciting on the premises, etc.).*
- Standards of conduct (expectations regarding punctuality, disciplinary procedures, and the complaint process, including your whistle-blower protection policy, your conflict-of-interest policy and code of ethics, policies regarding accepting fees and honoraria, relations with outside contractors, etc.).*
- Ending employment (process for resignation, grounds and process for involuntary termination, exit-interview process).
- An appendix of materials about the museum (organizational chart, fact sheet, list of board members, list of staff members, strategic plan, annual report, emergency plan, opening and closing procedures, security procedures, intern and/or volunteer handbook, etc.).*
- An appendix of materials about standards and best practices, such as the American Association of Museums' "Characteristics of Excellence for U.S. Museums."*
- An appendix of administrative forms the employee will need (conflict-of-interest form, time sheet, leave request form, mileage and expense reimbursement form, emergency contact information form, etc.). Note that should you need to create such forms, templates for many of them are available for free with Microsoft Office and online and can be adapted to your needs.*
- Employee acknowledgement form (a form indicating that employees have received and read the manual and agree to comply with it during their employment).*

Small organizations without paid staff often first prepare a volunteer orientation manual and later develop a staff handbook when paid employees join the team. A volunteer orientation manual can become a basis for later developing a board orientation manual, a personnel handbook, and an intern manual, as the organization grows. If each of these manuals follows the same general outline, it will be easier to update them all as many of the components will be similar and some will be identical, such as the brief history of the museum, copy of the strategic plan, and organizational chart. Such a manual should be a ready reference for everyone associated with the museum. It can complement and reinforce what is learned in a general volunteer or new employee orientation session, docent-training class, or board orientation session. Manuals should be written in such a way that, in the interest of transparency, they can be shared with volunteers, members, or anyone who requests one.

The components of the manual should live on a computer at your museum, and the format and binding should lend itself to easy and low-cost updating. The components of the manual also should be reviewed periodically and then updated by the board secretary or a designated administrator. Some, but not many, small museums have password-protected sections of their websites that contain important policies and procedures.

Job Descriptions

Developing written job descriptions for all employees, volunteers, board officers, board members, committee chairs, and everyone else who is part of your museum's team is a very important and effective way to clearly and formally define roles, responsibilities, and expectations. Without clearly defined roles, people often do not know whom they report to or what they are specifically supposed to do, and there can be much wasted and duplicated effort and confusion.

A job description typically contains

- title of the position;
- who the employee reports to;
- position summary;
- listing of major specific duties;
- knowledge, skills, training and experience (minimal requirements);
- salary range for the position.

Sample job descriptions for an executive director of a small to midsize museum and a volunteer docent are included in textboxes 2.1 and 2.2. It is a good practice for boards of directors to delineate clearly in the job description that it is the responsibility of the director to oversee the day-to-day operations of the museum.

Museum Job Descriptions and Organization Charts, edited by Mary Lister and Roxana Adams, provides additional examples of an array of types of museum job descriptions. (See "Print Publications" in the resource section at the end of this chapter.) In addition, job descriptions are posted in the job announcements sections of the websites of organization such as the American Association for State and Local History, the American Association of Museums, and regional museum associations, such as the Association of Midwest Museums. Other websites that feature museum position announcements/job descriptions include www.globalmuseum.org and www.museum-employment.org.

EXAMPLE JOB DESCRIPTION: OBERLIN HERITAGE CENTER EXECUTIVE DIRECTOR

REPORTS TO: Board of Trustees

Position Summary

In compliance with the mission statement and in collaboration with the board, the executive director is responsible for the management of Oberlin Heritage Center. The executive director implements board policy with the assistance of committees, staff, and key volunteers. Responsibilities include cataloging, preservation, and interpretation of Oberlin Heritage Center's collections and buildings; managing the board-approved annual budget; managing volunteers and staff; and ensuring proper record keeping. Specific duties include the following:

- Developing and implementing public programs and the annual membership meeting in cooperation with the Education and Program Committee of the board
- Overseeing the organization's on-site public tour program
- Overseeing the processing, cataloging, preservation, interpretation, and exhibition of the collection in accordance with museum standards
- Ensuring accurate maintenance of membership, donations, and board records
- Approving and managing special projects within budget constraints
- Selecting, training, supervising, and evaluating staff and student interns
- Recruiting, training, and managing volunteers and maintaining a docent manual
- Overseeing the preparation and distribution of the newsletter and publicity for Oberlin Heritage Center activities
- Advising on building preservation issues
- Researching and preparing grant applications for projects that support Oberlin Heritage Center's mission
- Preparing and submitting yearly budget proposals to the Finance Committee
- Working with board committees to recommend committee objectives and accomplishments in accordance with the strategic plan
- Representing Oberlin Heritage Center at community and professional events
- Keeping informed of new developments in the historical society and museum fields

(continued)

TEXTBOX 2.1 *(Continued)*

Knowledge, Skills, Training, Experience
- Minimum of a bachelor's degree, with a master's in history or a related field preferred
- Ability to work cooperatively with the board, members, volunteers, staff, and others to implement the mission of Oberlin Heritage Center
- Ability to represent Oberlin Heritage Center in creating appropriate partnerships with allied organizations
- Proven leadership and organizational skills
- Proven excellent verbal and written communication skills
- Computer proficiency with Microsoft Office
- Ability to network with regional and national historic organizations
- Demonstrated ability to work independently, and be self-motivated, yet function effectively within a team
- Experience in local historic administration, collections management, and historic preservation
- Experience in volunteer management

Salary Surveys and Benchmarking

When you are planning to create and fill a new staff position or to fill a position held by someone for many years, it is often useful to do some benchmarking to see what other nonprofit organizations and small museums in your region and elsewhere offer for comparable positions. Examine other similar positions, including what salaries and benefits they offer and what the job description entails, as a point of reference. Some statewide, regional, and national museums and nonprofit associations conduct periodic salary surveys to assess what compensation and benefits are offered by organizations of various budget sizes and in cities of various population sizes. For example, the June 1, 2009, Association of Midwest Museums Salary Survey reported that the average base pay for the executive director/CEO/president of the forty-seven museums it surveyed that had a budget of under $500,000 was $55,156.[2] Small museums not able to afford such a salary might instead elect to hire a part-time professional director or an office manager to help coordinate the work of the volunteers.

Volunteer Job Descriptions

Volunteer positions of all varieties (including board officers and members and committee chairs) should also have written job descriptions that outline

EXAMPLE VOLUNTEER JOB DESCRIPTION: WALK-IN OR GROUP TOUR DOCENT

REPORTS TO: Museum Education and Tour Coordinator
TERM: Docents must give at least four tours per year to remain active

Qualifications
The most important characteristics of an Oberlin Heritage Center docent are an interest in Oberlin history, a belief in history's relevance to life today, and a desire to welcome visitors to our community! Docents must be able to courteously engage all visitors and enthusiastically represent the Oberlin Heritage Center. They should be prepared for periods of standing, walking, and stair climbing during tours. Docents should also feel comfortable in crowded and noisy situations and be able to speak in a loud and clear voice.

Responsibilities
1. Prospective docents must first go on at least one tour of the Oberlin Heritage Center before attending docent training. A complimentary tour ticket for this purpose is available from the Museum Education and Tour Coordinator.
2. Prospective docents must fill out a volunteer application form, meet with the Museum Education and Tour Coordinator for an informational interview, and sign the Docent Agreement Form. The Oberlin Heritage Center may contact references and conduct a criminal background check.
3. Prospective docents must attend docent training, read the Oberlin Heritage Center docent manual, observe tours given by experienced docents, give a practice tour, and receive feedback.
4. Active docents must lead or help on a tour at least four times per year. This may include walk-in or group tours through the three historic buildings at the Oberlin Heritage Center, giving a room tour during special events, or helping on a walking tour.
5. Docents must attend Oberlin Heritage Center docent meetings and programs as their schedules permit.
6. Docents must have a neat appearance and dress in appropriate attire. A watch or time piece should be carried so that the docent may be mindful of the tour's time frame.

(continued)

TEXTBOX 2.2 (*Continued*)

7. Docents must arrive at least fifteen minutes early for tours to learn about tour changes or specific visitor needs. Docents must notify staff if they are unable to keep their prescheduled tour assignment.
8. Docents must record volunteer hours in the provided notebooks.
9. Docents must greet tour guests and properly receive and record tour payments (if trained to do so).
10. Docents must strive to engage visitors, especially youths, through conversation and available hands-on activities.
11. Docents must honestly answer visitor questions to the best of their ability and seek staff help if they are unable to do so.
12. Docents must properly handle furnishings and objects at the Oberlin Heritage Center and ensure that visitors are doing so as well.
13. Docents must review procedures and be prepared for emergency situations.
14. Docents must inform staff of any problems encountered during tours.
15. Docents must be willing to have their tour content, length, and presentation style evaluated by staff.
16. Docents should be prepared to do other tasks as requested if visitors do not come for walk-in tours.
17. Docents must request tour guests to submit tour feedback, thank visitors for coming, and encourage them to return with friends and family.

responsibilities and indicate who the volunteer reports to. Reviewing this job description with prospective volunteers during the recruitment process helps ensure that they and those they report to fully understand the commitment they are making and the assignment they are accepting. This will help to avoid misunderstandings and help volunteers understand their role within the organization. For example, a volunteer docent who is not given a written job description may not fully understand that he or she is expected to give three tours per month on a regular schedule. Without a written job description, the docent might not understand that he or she reports directly to the museum tour coordinator and should go to that person with questions or scheduling issues rather than to the head of the docent committee, the office manager, or some other individual.

A SYMBIOTIC RELATIONSHIP:
A VOLUNTEER IN A KEY STAFF ROLE

This story, from the Judah L. Magnes Museum (now the Magnes Collection of Jewish Art and Life at the Bancroft Library, University of California, Berkeley), demonstrates how one skilled and trained volunteer helped the museum in its journey to accomplish its mission. Susan S. Morris, former archivist and museum director, shares her experience of a small museum's effective use of a volunteer working in a key staff position.

To Set the Stage
The museum's mission: Collect, preserve, exhibit art and artifacts reflecting the diversity and complexity of the Jewish experience. Foster dialogue and explore links between Jewish and other cultures.

The mission shaped the shared goals and job descriptions of the small museum's paid staff and dedicated group of volunteers. The mission focused budget and fundraising. Resources to fully fund staff positions to accomplish goals were limited, so volunteers were essential in carrying out the mission. Volunteers were docents, fundraisers, and outreach educators. Retired librarians assisted the professional staff in the library and archives.

Passionate about the museum's collections and mission, the founding director established the culture of the museum by hiring individuals who shared his vision and commitment. Part of that culture included the lunch table, which was shared by staff and volunteers alike. The informal discussion around the lunch table involved enthusiastic participation from both volunteers and staff and typically focused on exhibits, visitor comments, collection issues, museum challenges, and creative solutions. There was a sense of camaraderie and shared delight as we worked together to keep this small museum engaging and professional.

Enter the Volunteer in a Key Staff Role
Museum member Herb Singer had just retired from his vocation as a social worker. However, he had not retired from his avocation as an expert craftsman repairing, rebuilding, and making violins. Herb made an appointment to learn about the museum volunteer program. During the course of the interview, an opportunity was seized, and both the needs of the museum and of the volunteer were served. A symbiotic relationship was created.

(*continued*)

TEXTBOX 2.3 (*Continued*)

Herb described his skills in using his hands, his love of detailed work in terms of measurement, working with delicate materials, and aesthetic symmetry. The interviewer observed that Herb was an active learner, appreciated the scope of the collections, and understood reasons for the collection-handling and security policies. Though the exhibit designer had not been looking for a volunteer exhibition preparator, Herb's skills and interest prompted a trial volunteer job as an assistant to the installation team. A new volunteer job description was created that fit Herb's considerable experience with fine woodworking and matched those skills with museum needs.

Initially, the job description entailed assisting with the measurement and mounting of prints, drawings, photographs, or archival documents. As Herb's skills grew, the job description grew organically, and he became an integral part of the exhibition mounting team. Having a highly skilled, dedicated volunteer in a key staff role reduced the exhibition budget considerably.

The exhibition team provided ongoing training and supervision. Herb clearly enjoyed his job and explored ways to do it better and more efficiently. He learned proper handling of objects, became skilled in returning objects to collection storage with even better archival matting and housing than before, and built frames and custom archival housing for the collections. Over time he became invaluable to the staff, and his suggestions and recommendations were respected and discussed. The scope of Herb's responsibilities and the hours worked grew organically as the relationship between the staff and the volunteer matured.

Outstanding as Herb's work as volunteer exhibit preparator and archival housing preparator were, there were noteworthy limits to the scope and responsibility of his job. Museum policies, including references to insurance regulations and legal liability, restricted the jobs a volunteer could perform. Additionally, Herb chose to take vacations when his skills were not needed; however, the museum could not require him to do so.

Lessons Learned
- Think outside the box.
- Look beyond a prospective volunteer's work experience or educational degree to match interests, skills, and intellectual curiosity to meet the museum's specific needs.
- Seize the opportunity.
- Allow for growth in volunteers' skills and interests.

The symbiotic relationship between the museum staff and a volunteer in a key staff position can be an important tool in the journey to achieving mission.

Volunteers Who Perform Key Staff Functions

Often in small museums, specific job assignments are undertaken very effectively by carefully selected volunteers. For example, a retiree with editing and publishing experience could be a great newsletter editor. A community-minded neighborhood resident could assume responsibility for mowing the grass regularly. A photography enthusiast could take photographs at special events and edit the photos to post on the organization's website. Other volunteers with specific skills could be called upon to help occasionally; for instance, a former English teacher could be asked to review and edit, or even help prepare, grant proposals. One well-organized and personable volunteer can often be an effective volunteer or docent coordinator or scheduler. Often a volunteer with retail or business experience can be a volunteer museum store manager.

For example, at the Lynden Pioneer Museum in Washington, the director/curator is the only paid full-time position, and there are a few ten-hour-per-week paid positions: gift shop coordinator, membership coordinator, custodian, and volunteer coordinator. The paid positions are primarily ones that entail some financial responsibilities. The organization is heavily dependent on an extensive array of volunteers filling many different assignments. Without them, the museum could not be open six or seven days a week. Volunteer staff positions that

Photo 2.3. Volunteers work as exhibit staff, installing outdoor exhibits and learning the art of making a stone arch at the Canal Center in Delphi, Indiana. (Courtesy of Dan McCain, Wabash & Erie Canal Association)

VOLUNTEERS IN KEY STAFF ROLES: FROM THE (ALL-)VOLUNTEER PERSPECTIVE

All the key staff roles at the Wabash & Erie Canal Center in Delphi, Indiana, are filled by volunteers and filled so effectively that the organization won the AASLH Corey Award in 2006. Although this chapter is dedicated to managing paid staff, this perspective from an all-volunteer organization provides insights into what is important for volunteers who act as staff. The following description of the Canal Center's operations was written by Dan McCain, who served as president in 2010.

Working with volunteers is better when they know they are trusted and admired—and even better if the coordinator is one of them. Their work as a volunteer is usually an extension of their career or their hobbies.

At the Canal Center, volunteers tackle innovative exhibits for indoors or outside. The challenge is to excite potential volunteers early by bringing exhibit ideas in for their consultation. The potential of doing almost any size project is there if you have a motivated crew.

We began with a myriad of projects developed by a professional museum planner. He could make drawings that our volunteers could follow. Our crew of up to a dozen retirees has carried out a regular Monday-Wednesday-Friday schedule throughout the last fourteen years. The nice part is that we just work mornings. We don't get together to drink coffee and chatter—we come to work. One volunteer calls this "job security."

We handle challenges of how to do a specific task. We form a circle, and whoever has the most knowledge or experience in a process or use of some different material gets the most notice. A consensus decision develops. If for some reason that decision wasn't the best solution, nobody points their finger in disgust. The group's appreciation for consensus decisions prevails. There is respect for good experience no matter if it comes from the coordinator or a member of the group.

We have enjoyed getting expert technical advice from specialists—even from hundreds of miles away. One example is a college instructor from central Michigan who comes as a volunteer and brings his wife. He tutors us on metal restoration. Learning from a master is fun and stimulating. Developing a skill like riveting or straightening bent beams is something we can say we know how to do. We have completely restored two old iron bridges that were erected over the canal as trail bridges.

Several projects have challenged us with masonry issues. Once, the building of a sizable stone arch for creating our Lime Kiln exhibit brought us a volunteer mason from the Chicago area. He worked with us several times each for several days, teaching us how to make forms and lay the stone arch to perfection. We love learning new skills and showing the public what volunteers can do when they are motivated.

■

report to the director include a registrar, archivist, maintenance worker, program coordinator, and publicity person. Volunteers in this case are treated essentially as unpaid staff and are expected to adhere to all policies and procedures.[3]

In cases where everyone at the museum is a volunteer, often one super-volunteer or the board president is the top person in charge. This can work very well. But just as when there is paid staff, confusion can reign when it is not clear who is responsible for what or who is in charge. Turf wars can wreak havoc. Sometimes long-entrenched volunteers are uninterested in welcoming newcomers to the group. It is important to have well-thought-out processes for recruiting, training, retaining, and evaluating volunteers, a volunteer orientation manual, written job descriptions for all positions, and an organizational chart that shows the chain of command between the various volunteers, committee chairs, and board members to delineate roles.

Sometimes museums are fortunate to acquire a half-time or full-time "volunteer" who is sometimes paid a stipend or minimum wage for a set period by a governmental service or job-training program. In such situations, often the individual is required to comply with personnel requirements and procedures of the outside sponsoring organization. In this case, the job description often needs to be developed to suit the requirements of both the host site and the sponsoring organization. For example, at the Oberlin Heritage Center, a federally funded job-training program for low-income senior citizens called Mature Services, Inc., has provided half-time employees to serve as building and grounds assistants and front desk receptionists. In such cases, the director works closely with the representative of the sponsoring agency to develop a job description and to provide daily supervision, with periodic visits from the agency representative to assure that all requirements are being met. The Oberlin Heritage Center also hosted an AmeriCorps volunteer for ten months as part of an Ohio Historical Society initiative to place interns in host sites throughout the state to coordinate activities related to the 150th anniversary of the Civil War.

Hiring the Most Qualified Person for the Job

Publicizing the Job Opportunity

After developing a carefully crafted job description, publicize the job vacancy at the museum, in your own newsletter, on your website, and in the community (at the public library and on community bulletin boards) as well as through free online website job postings and through the career services offices of academic institutions in your area. Lengthy newspaper advertisements are very costly and may not yield great results. Select, paid postings on career boards on professional organizations' websites, such as the American Association for State and Local History (AASLH) and the American Association of Museums (AAM), may be worthwhile, depending on the nature of the position and whether you seek to attract a national pool of applicants.

Including in the job posting an established date by which applications should be received is advisable so that you can then begin screening them all at once. State where the application materials should be submitted and whether you prefer to receive them by U.S. mail, fax, or e-mail. Request that each applicant provide a cover letter and a resume. The cover letter can be useful in assessing the applicant's writing skills and knowledge of how to prepare business correspondence. Also, ask for names and contact information for three work-related references. You may also wish to ask the applicant to complete an application-for-employment form, which is a good place to include questions such as the following:

- Do you have a valid driver's license (if driving is required for the position)?
- In the past seven years, have you been convicted of a felony? If so, please explain.
- Are you legally eligible for employment in the United States?

See appendix A for a sample job application form.

Job Search Record Keeping

Create a separate folder for each applicant for the position and keep that person's resume, application, and other materials there, along with a cover tracking sheet for ready reference, where notes of all contacts regarding the candidate and his or her application can be recorded. For example,

8/16   Received application.
8/27   Judy Smith phoned applicant and set up interview for 9/5 at 10 a.m.
9/3   Applicant called and provided contact information for three references.

This will make it easy to track and follow up on job candidates throughout the search process.

Screening, Interviewing, and Rating Applicants

The materials submitted by the applicants should be screened as objectively as possible. You may wish to devise a rating chart for your search committee or hiring team members to score applicants on how well they meet or exceed the criteria in the job description. The search committee should include the executive director or board president and the person who will be directly supervising the employee. See appendix B for a sample application-rating form.

It often works well with a large pool of applicants to do an initial screening and remove from consideration those who do not meet the minimum criteria. Then, assess the remaining applications and select five to ten of the best for phone interviews, asking each candidate the same set of predetermined interview questions. Complete a summary sheet on each phone interview. The phone interviews will help to decide upon a small group of finalists (three to five) whom you will invite to come in for in-person interviews. Should you have candidates coming from some distance, it is desirable to offer them an honorarium to help cover their travel expenses or to reimburse them for the actual costs.

Great care should be taken throughout the interview process to adhere to equal opportunity and affirmative action guidelines and to avoid any potentially discriminatory language or inappropriate or illegal questions, for instance, about the candidate's children, day-care arrangements, religion, marital status, or age. (See the section on human resources in chapter 4 of Book 2 in this series.)

In interviewing finalists for a management position, it is often helpful to have one person ask the predetermined set of questions and at least one other person present to observe, listen, and also take part in the interviews. In that way you will have two perspectives on the candidate's performance during the interview. Asking job candidates to tell you about what they most enjoyed and learned from a recent (or not so recent) visit to another museum or cultural attraction can also provide interesting insights. Asking how they found out about the current opportunity and why they are interested in the position can also be enlightening.

Whether candidates have taken the time to learn about your museum ahead of time and their impressions of its challenges and opportunities can also be revealing. For management positions, big-picture questions about current trends and hot issues in the museum field can also help to assess a candidate's broader knowledge and suitability for the position. Being an effective museum administrator typically requires solid professional training and expertise in the field. Each candidate has unique strengths and weaknesses and should be assessed fairly and independently, regardless of whom he or she knows or is related to within the community.

Depending on the position, you may wish to include a skills test of some kind, such as asking a candidate for a fundraising assistant position to spend fifteen minutes on the computer writing a letter to a potential donor asking for a contribution to your annual fund (using a handout with the basic facts). Or, to assess a museum educator candidate's interpretive skills, give him an artifact and some basic facts about it. Then give him ten minutes to develop a brief presentation on how he might interpret this artifact for a school group. In these ways you can quickly assess candidates' communication skills and ability to perform under pressure.

Devise a plan ahead of time to make the most of candidates' time with you so that they will have an opportunity to fully understand what the position entails and to get acquainted with the organization, the facility, and the community, and you will have an opportunity to assess their suitability for the position. You might include a tour of the facility and brief meetings with key staff and volunteers. Be sure to include time for the applicant to ask questions.

When you conclude the interview, let applicants know what will happen next and when they will hear from you. Then write up a summary, including strengths and weaknesses and any potential areas of concern.

Reference and Background Checks

In our increasingly litigious society, great care must be taken and common sense must be used to avoid undue risks, particularly when staff or volunteers will be interacting one-on-one with vulnerable individuals, such as children, nursing home residents, or the differently abled. Thorough reference checks and conversations with references should be conducted carefully and documented meticulously. Some museums conduct formal background checks, including fingerprinting and criminal record checks for all employees and volunteers. Others do this for new hires only or only for those who will have unsupervised direct interaction with vulnerable individuals.

Verification of academic degrees and employment records, as well as criminal and driving record searches, are sometimes included in the process. Some informal background checking can of course be done through Internet sites such as Google, LinkedIn, and Facebook.

Checking references from former employers and asking for a copy of applicants' most recent performance appraisal from their current or most recent position is essential. Asking references whether they would rehire the individual you are considering can be especially revealing. Nonprofit management websites and publications can provide sample work sheets to use in conducting reference checks.

Making the Decision

Assessment of your finalists and selection of your top candidates should be careful and methodical. Do take into consideration all the information and observations you and your team have made along the way. Did the candidate make a great first impression? Does the person's skill set and expertise match the job description? What unique qualities will she bring to the position? Does this individual bring ethnic, age, gender, or other types of diversity to enhance your team? What skills will she need to develop in order to do the job well? Does your intuition tell you about how her personality will fit within the organizational culture, and does she have the potential to become an effective and essential part of your team? Was she courteous to the people who greeted her at the front door? Was she professional in phone contacts and in her attire? Does she seem to have the flexibility and adaptability to function within your work setting? Would you be happy to have her represent your organization in this particular job category?

Employment Offers, Terms, and Negotiations

Once the finalists have been interviewed and rated and you have checked references and verified employment information, a verbal offer of employment can be extended to the top candidate, accompanied by a letter outlining all conditions and terms. It is courteous to give the candidate a few days to consider the offer. Some candidates will want to negotiate about salary, starting date, benefits, or other details. Thinking through how much you are willing to bend and knowing what if any leeway you have in the budget ahead of time will make it easier to respond in such situations.

In some cases, museums ask the executive director or other senior management employees to sign an employment contract for a specified period. In such a situation, it is not unreasonable for the candidate to ask for time to have an attorney review the contract. In other cases, employees are hired "at will," without a specified duration of employment. In this case, either the staff member or the employer can end the employment relationship at any time, without cause. Having a six-month probationary period for new employees is advisable as this allows both the employee and the employer to see whether the applicant is a good fit for the position.

Notifying Those Who Were Not Hired

Once an applicant has accepted the position, it is courteous and professional to notify the other applicants that they were not selected and to wish them well in their future endeavors. State that you will keep their application materials on file. Application materials for all candidates should be kept in your secure human resources files in accordance with your records retention and destruction policy. (If you do not have such a policy, your accountant or financial advisor can assist in developing one.) It is also critical to develop and maintain secure, well-organized personnel records for all employees and to store them in a locked filing cabinet. This will be the place to keep employment paperwork, payroll documents, performance appraisals, records of any disciplinary actions or promotions, training records, wage and salary actions, employee benefit papers, letters of reference or commendation, exit interview forms, and the like. In many states, employees may ask to see a copy of their personnel file at any time.

New Person on Board—Now What?

Plan an orientation strategy for new employees to help them become part of the team and to get the right start in their new position. Develop a checklist of items that should be covered with each new employee. Having different members of the team tackle different parts of the orientation can help new employees get acquainted with more people and feel welcome more quickly.

As a new staff member, being a good listener is crucial, especially in your three-month honeymoon period. Ask your colleagues what they wish they had known about the museum before they joined the board or became a staff member or volunteer. Inquire what new thing they have learned about the organization in the last year. Let others know that you value their opinion, that their support is essential, and that you appreciate both.

Encourage a newly hired executive director arriving on the scene to take the time to familiarize him- or herself with the existing personnel (volunteer, staff, and board) and to get to know the institutional culture before implementing radical change. He or she should be encouraged to take the time to make an appointment and sit down individually with each and every board member, staff member, and key volunteer to get acquainted, ask them what they do at the museum, and find out about their hopes and dreams for the institution. These conversations will go a long way toward building a great first impression and getting key players to work as a team. This should also help provide the new director with critical information about the organization's beginnings and history and may help him or her learn to use this information to inspire others to get engaged in the museum's work.

Unless the board has presented a new director with a clear plan of work for the first few months on the job, he or she may consider devising a short-term draft plan to present to the board based upon the individual meetings.

Evaluating Employees

Conducting an evaluation of new employees at the end of their six-month probationary period and conducting an annual evaluation of the work of each staff member (and, ideally, each key volunteer) provides a good opportunity for an open and constructive dialogue. Usually, the executive director or direct supervisor evaluates the work of each paid staff member, while the work of the executive director is evaluated by the board president or executive committee. Some supervisors first ask employees to fill out a self-assessment form, which the supervisor then reviews. Care should be taken to tie assessments to employees' job description and to assess performance based on the duties and expectations outlined therein. See appendix C for a sample employee evaluation form.

The employee and the supervisor then meet to go over the assessment. This is a wonderful opportunity to thank the employee for accomplishments during the year, discuss areas for improvement, and establish priorities for the coming year. It is also an opportunity for the supervisor to get feedback about what the employee may need to be more effective in his or her job and to talk about professional development possibilities for the coming year. In evaluating the executive director, the board or governing authority should review his or her performance based upon the executive director's job description and effectiveness in implementing the organization's strategic plans and initiatives. Examples of staff evaluation forms can be found in many nonprofit management publications.

Providing feedback on an employee's (or volunteer's) performance should not be limited to the annual review but should take place in a variety of ways throughout the year. Giving praise, showing appreciation for work well done, and providing constructive criticism where appropriate should be an ongoing process that is part of open communication between the supervisor and the employee or volunteer.

Taking the time to let people know you appreciate their great work in a timely manner builds a strong relationship. There are many ways to do this: an in-person thank-you, a handwritten note, and mention of latest successes at meetings are a few simple ideas. When making a suggestion for improvement, try to start positively, showcasing something the employee did well before moving into the constructive criticism: "I greatly appreciate your finishing the grant report on time. However, there are a number of typos that need to be corrected, and that is going to slow us down in getting this out the door. In the future, please proofread your work more thoroughly or ask a coworker to do it before making twenty copies. This will save us all time in the long run."

Dealing with Performance Issues

Addressing challenges in job performance is an important part of the annual evaluation process. However, performance and conduct issues will arise in any work setting from time to time. Generally, performance issues arise when the individual is not completing the duties outlined in the job description. Often these situations can be addressed through supervision and training. Conduct issues such as repeated absenteeism, dress code violations, insubordination, or alcohol or drug issues must often be handled by disciplinary action. The supervisor should address problems that arise with an employee in a timely, fair, consistent, professional, and confidential manner that focuses on the goal of staff improvement and is in accordance with all policies.

The key to dealing with employee performance problems is to document carefully, in writing, any and all incidents that could lead to a disciplinary action. For example, if the part-time receptionist or librarian, who is scheduled to work from 9 a.m. to 12 p.m. on Wednesdays and Fridays, repeatedly arrives twenty minutes late, call this to his attention and write a note to add to his personnel file, describing what happened and when. In cases such as conduct or safety violations or absenteeism, a written warning should be given and discussed with the employee, then signed and dated by both the employee and the supervisor.

Getting legal advice in any situation involving potential for an employee's dismissal is strongly recommended. Voluntary termination (where the employee quits on his or her own) is generally preferable to involuntary termination mandated by the employer and is less apt to lead to lengthy and costly legal action.

Professional Development

Each employee, volunteer, and board member should be given opportunities to increase and enhance his or her skills. Building an institutional culture where all are working to improve their knowledge and strengthen the institution helps build morale and an environment that values professionalism and learning. Providing frequent and varied opportunities for staff, board members, and volunteers to develop their own professional skills is an essential way to build organizational capacity and can be done in a variety of creative and low-cost ways. People are much more likely to stay longer if they feel they are given opportunities for personal and professional growth and if they feel their work is appreciated as part of an overall team approach to accomplish organizational goals.

Many museums offer periodic field trips to other museums and cultural attractions as an excellent way for museum personnel (board, staff, and volunteer) to get to know one another better and find new ideas and inspiration. Bringing in an outside program presenter to address topics that your museum needs to

Photo 2.4. Oberlin Heritage Center docents and staff enjoy a day away at another historic site or community each year, offering volunteers and staff a chance to get to know one another, learn how another museum functions, and gain insights about their own tour techniques. After visiting the Spirit of '76 Museum and lunch, they enjoyed a walking tour of downtown Wellington, Ohio. (Courtesy of Oberlin Heritage Center)

learn more about can be an excellent way to develop in-house skills and build relationships with people from nearby institutions. For example, consider bringing in an outside speaker and hosting a workshop on how to apply for a Humanities Council or Arts Council grant or offering a training session on how to use PastPerfect collections management software.

Developing the museum skills and professionalism of your board, volunteers, interns, and paid staff should be an ongoing process. Ask for help from others in the nonprofit world. For example, call up the volunteer coordinator of a nearby museum with an effective volunteer program and ask if you could take the coordinator to lunch to pick his or her brain about effective strategies to manage volunteers and strengthen your own program.

Become a member of museum service and professional organizations and read their newsletters and publications. Create a "routing slip" and pass the AASLH's *History News* or the AAM's *Museum* magazine around so key members of your team can take it home and peruse the latest issues for relevant articles. Subscribe to *The Chronicle of Philanthropy* or read it at your library to stay on top of the latest developments. Join the Society for Nonprofit Organizations, and six times a year you will receive *Nonprofit World*, a helpful publication that contains many short articles such as "Add Energy and Diversity to Your Organization with Interns" and "Can We Call a Truce? Tips for Negotiating Workplace Conflicts." The Center for the Future of Museums' free e-newsletter is another great way to stay on top of trends and gain new ideas.

Consider adding a ten- to fifteen-minute educational component to each and every staff meeting, board meeting, volunteer meeting, or docent meeting on a topic of current interest that will help attendees develop the knowledge they need to fulfill their roles as part of the team. For example, have an executive director from another nonprofit organization in your region that has recently completed a successful capital campaign come in and talk about how they did it. Or have an accountant give a presentation on what changes nonprofit organizations are expected to make in their policies and procedures, financial practices, and record keeping in the aftermath of the Sarbanes-Oxley legislation. Webinars are also becoming more accessible and popular, and several people can sit around one computer to learn together. Another possibility would be to ask a staff member to research and develop a brief presentation on a topic you all need to learn more about. This could be given both at a staff meeting and at a board meeting.

Some professional organizations, such as the AAM's Small Museum Administrators Committee and the AASLH Small Museums Committee, as well as training programs like the Seminar for Historical Administration and the Getty Museum Leadership Institute, occasionally provide scholarships to museum professionals from small museums to attend conferences, trainings, webinars, and workshops. While these may not cover all expenses, they can often put such an opportunity more within reach financially. Serving as program presenter at professional conferences is a great way to develop skills and to network and also helps to build a stronger resume.

Small museum professionals can also gain considerable expertise and knowledge by serving on the boards of statewide or regional museum associations or other nonprofit organizations in their community, such as the chamber of commerce or visitors' bureau. Taking part in a city- or countywide, yearlong leadership training program could also benefit museum staff and provide great opportunities for relationship building and networking outside the museum field.

Small museum professionals can also develop considerable knowledge about human resource management and professional standards and broaden their knowledge of the museum field by serving as a peer reviewer for the AAM's Museum Assessment or Accreditation programs or for grant proposals from the Institute of Museum and Library Services, the National Endowment for the Humanities, and other such funding agencies.

Standards, Best Practices, and Other Great Resources

Reinventing the wheel in the arena of human resources administration is not necessary. Though R&D stands for "research and development" in private industry, in the world of small, nonprofit organizations, many use the acronym tongue-in-cheek to stand for "rip off and duplicate." Seeking ideas, inspiration, and advice from your partners in the small museum field and from other nonprofits and professional organizations, such as your statewide or regional museum association or a statewide nonprofit association, is not only acceptable but also smart. Likewise, board members and volunteers who work with other organizations and publications such as this one can provide examples of policies and procedures, forms, and documents from comparable organizations that can be useful in devising your own.

As in all areas of museum administration, becoming familiar with accepted standards and best practices in the field can be very helpful in the arena of human resources. The AASLH's new Standards and Excellence Program for History Organizations (StEPs) can help the museum chart a course of improvement. Going through this self-assessment process using the "Management" and "Mission, Vision, and Governance" sections can assist in delineating responsibilities and assuring that the board, staff, and volunteers work cooperatively to accomplish their mission. Small museums may also derive great benefit from structured guidance offered by a peer reviewer through the AAM's Museum Assessment Program (MAP).

The Oberlin Heritage Center had a MAP institutional assessment done in the mid-1990s, two years after hiring its first executive director. The peer reviewer made a number of helpful recommendations about human resource management and governance. Among them, he noted that an organizational chart should be developed to define who reports to whom and a board manual should be put in place establishing the board's roles and responsibilities and its relationship to the staff and volunteers. He also emphasized that the director should be given more authority over the daily operations. His recommendations were incorporated into the organization's strategic plan and implemented successfully, leading to a stronger organization with a clearer delineation of authority.

Some museums use the StEPs and MAP programs as stepping-stones toward eventually becoming accredited by the AAM. AAM accreditation is generally accepted as the gold standard in the museum world. Museums that become accredited have successfully demonstrated adherence to the AAM Characteristics of Excellence for U.S. Museums, which are outlined on the AAM website. Including these characteristics in both the formal "museum-speak" and the "plain-language" versions, which AAM also provides, can be a very useful addition to your personnel, volunteer, and board orientation manuals, whether or not your museum is accredited. Several relate to human resource administration, such as "The governing authority, staff, and volunteers have a clear and shared understanding of their roles and responsibilities" and "The museum strives to be inclusive and offers opportunities for diverse participation."[4]

The Oberlin Heritage Center began working to become accredited in the mid-1990s and achieved accreditation in 2005. The process required the participation of the entire team of staff, volunteers, and board members and brought them together working under the leadership of the executive director toward this ambitious goal. The accreditation process entailed a thorough review of all aspects of the museum's operations, including human resources, management, and governance policies and procedures, as well as the development of many new ones. It was a great learning experience for the staff, board, and volunteers. It also helped foster a much greater appreciation for museum standards and best practices and an institutional culture of continuous improvement. The executive director believes that in many respects it was the most challenging and most rewarding undertaking that the museum has accomplished in its recent history.

In addition to the MAP and Accreditation programs, AAM also provides many other resources for museums. These include professional conferences and seminars, as well as a new series of webinars with titles like "HR Basics: Evaluating and Coaching Employees" and "Museum Standards and Best Practices Primer."

Becoming familiar with, and striving to attain and adhere to, standards and best practices for the nonprofit sector in general can also be very useful, particularly in the human resources arena. For example, *The Standards for Excellence: An Ethics and Accountability Code for the Nonprofit Sector* is a very useful reference. It addresses fifty-five performance standards in eight principle areas: mission and program, governing body, conflict of interest, human resources, financial and legal, openness, fundraising, and public affairs and public policy. These standards can be used as the basis for an organizational self-assessment and as an effective professional development tool for staff, board members, and volunteers. Several states have adopted state-specific versions of the standards and offer periodic training and resources and a certification process for organizations wishing to work toward improving their policies and achieving the standards (see Standards for Excellence Institute website in the resource section at the end of this chapter). Consider including a copy of the *Standards for Excellence* in your personnel, volunteer, and board orientation manuals as a ready reference for accepted best practices.

Understanding where your museum is in its evolution can help you to assess your situation and plan a strong course of action to help move your organization forward. One straightforward way to do this is outlined in the book *The 5 Life Stages of Nonprofit Organizations: Where You Are, Where You're Going, and What to Expect When You Get There* (see "Print Publications" below). This assessment can be done by an individual or group and can provide a helpful framework for discussion. A brief online assessment of your organization is offered by the publisher of the book at the website www.fieldstonealliance.org under "Free Resources." You may well find that many of the issues you now face are very similar to those faced by other nonprofit organizations at a similar stage of development. This resource provides specific strategies for executive directors and boards to help address their challenges. Many tremendous nonprofit resources can also be found online, offering sample documents, forms, and templates for most management needs (see "Web Resources").

While finding examples from elsewhere is a great starting point, do take the time to develop, implement, and customize policies and procedures that are suited to your own organization. It is always advisable to have an attorney review any policies or documents you devise to assure that you are in compliance with all applicable laws. Seek out attorneys who might work pro bono for your organization or include funding for these services in your budget.

Conclusion

Working as an administrator in a small museum environment requires determination, flexibility, passion, and people skills. Building the best team you can with the resources you have will help you and your museum to survive and thrive. Get the right people on board. Make sure they have the skills, tools, and information they need to do their jobs. Help them grow and succeed in their positions. Celebrate and recognize their accomplishments. The challenges are considerable, and the rewards are even greater. Enjoy the journey.

Resources

Print Publications

American Association of Museums (AAM). *2009 Museum Financial Information.* Washington, DC: AAM Press, 2009.

———. *Accreditation Resource Kit.* Washington, DC: AAM, 2006.

———. "Code of Ethics for Museums." AAM. 1993, 1999. www.aam-us.org/museumresources/ethics/coe.cfm (accessed May 15, 2011).

———. *National Standards and Best Practices for U.S. Museums.* Washington, DC: AAM, 2008.

———. *Small Museums and Accreditation: Sample Documents from Small Accredited Museums.* Washington, DC: AAM, 2007. CD-ROM available free of charge.

American Association for State and Local History (AASLH). *StEPs Workbook: Standards and Excellence Program for History Organizations.* Nashville, TN: AASLH, 2009.

Estrada, Daniel, Maris Stella (Star) Swift, and Timothy Chester. "Human Resources and E-Discovery Law: New Challenges in Museum Administration." *Association of Midwest Museums News Brief* 23, no. 3 (fall 2009): 1.

George, Gerald. *Starting Right: A Basic Guide to Museum Planning.* American Association for State and Local History Book Series. 2nd ed. Walnut Creek, CA: AltaMira Press, 2004.

Larson, Carl E., and Frank M. J. LaFasto. *TeamWork: What Must Go Right/What Can Go Wrong.* Newbury Park, CA: Sage Publications, 1989.

Lencioni, Patrick. *The Five Dysfunctions of a Team: A Leadership Fable.* San Francisco, CA: Jossey-Bass, 2002.

Lister, Mary, and Roxana Adams, eds. *Museum Job Descriptions and Organization Charts.* Washington, DC: American Association of Museums, 1999.

McMillan, Edward J. *Model Policies & Procedures for Not-for-Profit Organizations.* Hoboken, NJ: John Wiley & Sons, 2003.

Robinson, Andy. *Great Boards for Small Group: A 1-Hour Guide to Governing a Growing Nonprofit.* Medfield, MA: Emerson & Church, 2006.

Simon, Judith Shaken, with J. Terence Donovan. *The 5 Life Stages of Nonprofit Organizations: Where You Are, Where You're Going, and What to Expect When You Get There, Featuring the Wilder Nonprofit Life Stage Assessment.* St. Paul, MN: Fieldstone Alliance/Amherst H. Wilder Foundation, 2001.

Vineyard, Sue. *Recognizing Volunteers and Paid Staff.* Darien, IL: Heritage Arts Publishing, 2001.

Web Resources

American Association of Museums (www.aam-us.org): information about museum accreditation, "Characteristics of Excellence for U.S. Museums," "Characteristics of an Accredited Museum," and extensive resources for AAM members

American Association for Museum Volunteers (www.aamv.org): an organization for both professional volunteer coordinators and museum volunteers; includes a sample newsletter and other resources; AAMV members have access to a helpful active e-mail list about all aspects of volunteer management

American Association for State and Local History (www.aaslh.org): valuable information on succession planning, museum careers, professional development, and more

American Management Association (www.amanet.org): podcasts, articles, and free e-newsletters on various management topics; primarily geared to businesses but also helpful for nonprofit management

Board Café (www.boardcafe.org): free e-newsletter geared to board members but useful to executive directors as well

BoardSource (www.boardsource.org): resources and publications for nonprofit governance and management

Center for the Future of Museums (www.futureofmuseums.org): from the American Association of Museums, a great source of ideas and news for museum leaders and fans, both on the website and through a free e-newsletter

Fieldstone Alliance (www.fieldstonealliance.org): many helpful free articles and organizational self-assessment tools

Idealist.org (www.idealist.org): resources for volunteer managers

Independent Sector (www.independentsector.org): helpful articles for nonprofit leadership, some for a fee; free download of the booklet *Principles for Good Governance and Ethical Practice: A Guide for Charities and Foundations*, produced in 2007 by a panel on the nonprofit sector convened by Independent Sector

Free Management Library (www.managementhelp.org): a free online library of management resources for nonprofits and for-profits, including several helpful self-assessment tools

MAP for Nonprofits (www.mapfornonprofits.org): a terrific resource for all aspects of nonprofit governance and management

Minnesota Council of Nonprofits (www.mncn.org): extensive information about all aspects of nonprofit management

Nonprofit Good Practice (www.npgoodpractice.org): helpful resources on an array of nonprofit management and leadership topics from the Nonprofit Leadership Institute at Grand Valley State University in Allendale, Michigan

Serviceleader.org (www.serviceleader.org): many tips on volunteer recruitment and management

Society for Human Resource Management (www.shrm.org): extensive information, some accessible to members only

Society for Nonprofit Organizations (www.snpo.org): some articles from *Nonprofit World* magazine accessible at no charge, with more resources available to members

Standards for Excellence Institute (www.standardsforexcellenceinstitute.org): a useful tool for institutional management, *Standards for Excellence: An Ethics and Accountability Code for the Nonprofit Sector*

Notes

1. The fact sheet can also be the basis for developing the introductory section of a volunteer orientation manual or personnel handbook, and it can serve as a ready reference for board members who are out advocating for you in your community and speaking with prospective donors.

2. "Salary Survey," Association of Midwest Museums, June 1, 2009, 4.

3. E-mail from Troy Luginbill to the author, May 4, 2010.

4. "American Association of Museums (AAM) Accreditation Program Standards: Characteristics of an Accreditable Museum," AAM, December 3, 2004, www.aam-us.org/museumresources/accred/upload/Characteristics of an Accreditable Museum 1-1-05.pdf (accessed August 22, 2011).

CHAPTER THREE
ARE YOU BEING SERVED?
ATTRACTING AND KEEPING VOLUNTEERS
Patricia L. Miller

Museums of all types and sizes depend on volunteers to make their programs possible. Many museums were founded by volunteers, and some continue to be operated entirely by volunteers. Volunteers fill many functions, including greeting visitors, serving as guides or docents, helping with archival and object collections, leading educational programs, conducting outreach, assisting with planning and installing exhibits, providing legal and financial expertise, and assisting with emerging technology. Volunteers serve as unpaid but highly valued staff.

Museums may be the lucky recipients of gifts of time and talent freely offered by volunteers to assist with many tasks. As in other areas of operation, the planning and developing of a structured program for volunteers can establish mutual benefits for both the volunteers and the museums they support. Such a program should have its own goals and objectives, but it should build on the museum's mission and be incorporated into the museum's strategic planning. From recruitment to evaluation, museums can build successful programs that help make the contributions of volunteers more efficient and effective.

Types of Volunteer Support for Museums

The most important volunteer position in a museum is a seat on the governing board. Board membership requires dedication and commitment. It entails financial, legal, and ethical oversight, as well as attention to stewardship responsibilities for collections. While the board can delegate responsibilities, it must always know and understand what is going on. The board has an obligation to protect the museum from liability. Museum volunteers often outnumber staff members, so it is essential to establish clear guidelines for volunteers that meet legal requirements.

In a small museum where members of the board also serve as volunteers in other capacities, it is especially important to keep governing and operating roles separate, as they have different functions. In simple terms, the govern-

Photo 3.1. Volunteers shelving library materials. (Courtesy of Illinois Heritage Association)

ing board sets policies; staff and volunteers enact them. In a small museum, volunteers (including trustees) often perform functions that would be the responsibilities of staff in a larger institution. Establishing boundaries and putting things in writing can prevent a lot of misunderstandings. Trustee and volunteer manuals are helpful tools. A volunteer manual typically includes a fact sheet about the museum, an overview of the museum and the volunteer program, an organizational chart, an annual calendar of volunteer activities and training sessions, a statement of professional standards and ethics, and sample evaluation forms. In addition, the volunteer manual usually discusses the rewards and benefits of volunteering in the program, the responsibilities of volunteers and of the museum, museum security, emergency procedures, and personnel policies relating to volunteers.[1] The volunteer manual is very similar to a museum's personnel manual. (See the section on the personnel manual in chapter 2 of this book.)

Perhaps the most common role for a museum volunteer is as a guide or docent. The word "docent" comes from the Latin *docere*, which means "to teach" or "to instruct." Volunteer guides take visitors through exhibits and engage them in conversations about the stories the exhibits present. They are frontline ambassadors for the museum and also serve a security function. While some guides are little more than hosts or hostesses, using them as such misses an opportunity to have them fully present the museum. However, a meaningful interchange between guests and docents is not likely to happen without a structured training program. It requires some study to understand how to interact with many kinds of museum visitors and how to convey the themes of various exhibits. Experienced docents are treasures; they do not often continue to serve without some nurturing.

Volunteers may assist with formal educational programs. Teachers and retired teachers are excellent volunteers in this area, but one should not overlook someone without formal training who is especially interested in a topic. Volunteers lend their skills and expertise to hands-on activities and living history programs. They develop programs that meet state-mandated curriculum guidelines. They work in gardens and help with horticultural programs. They play vital roles in visitor services. They help with museum stores, sometimes operating them completely. Volunteers help with libraries and archives and assist with membership. They may participate in a speakers' bureau to help promote museum programs.

In today's world, volunteers are sometimes looking for a short-term commitment, often referred to as episodic volunteering. They may be attracted to a particular program or temporary exhibit, but they might be unwilling or unable to sign up for every Tuesday and Thursday afternoon for a year. It is necessary for museums to have a great deal of flexibility in scheduling to meet the needs of volunteers, and short-term volunteers have important roles to play. For instance, they might give an evening to working on a telephone tree for an annual giving campaign. People who are out of work in times of economic downturn can sometimes volunteer for short-term projects and gain valuable skills at the same time.

Volunteers also help museums in managing collections. They may serve on a collections committee, lending expertise to selecting proposed acquisitions and documenting collections. They may be trained to register and catalog artifacts, helping the museum to meet professional standards. They might get involved in ongoing research of collections. Such research could lead them into work on exhibits or publications.

Today's museums are required to meet far more legal and financial regulations than in earlier days. Volunteers with backgrounds in accounting, law, or business can help museums understand and follow accepted standards for nonprofit operation. Such volunteers might help a small museum with bookkeeping, auditing, or maintaining good financial practices, such as establishing a system for two people to handle money, making timely bank deposits, and avoiding cash transactions. Professional organizations such as Volunteer Lawyers for the Arts can help a museum find volunteers with these kinds of skills.[2]

Nontraditional Museum Volunteers

Youth Volunteers

Science and natural history museums, zoos, aquariums, and children's museums actively engage young people in volunteering. It is less common for youth volunteers to participate in small general museums, historic sites, or

Photo 3.2. Youth volunteers can help with many activities in museums. (Courtesy of Shannon Reddy, Miller Park Zoo, Decatur, Illinois)

house museums, but there are overlooked opportunities for young people to offer volunteer services in these venues. Any youth volunteer program needs solid planning and quite a bit of structure to ensure that the volunteers have a rewarding experience and contribute to the museum's operation. Youth volunteers are usually accepted at a museum at around age thirteen and can continue through high school. While some young people are motivated by school service requirements, more volunteer to follow some interest. They act as tour guides, greeters, assistants in educational programs, and "explainers," as well as serving in many other capacities. Youth volunteers generally need to have a parent sign a release form and may need references from a teacher, coach, or counselor. They typically have to commit to orientation and training and to volunteering a certain number of hours to the museum. Although not required to do so by law, a museum would be prudent to correlate its guidelines for youth volunteers with child labor laws.[3]

Family Volunteers

Museums can offer opportunities for families to spend some quality time together. Special events, such as historic celebrations, are appealing to families. Outdoor events, such as a cleanup day, might be inviting. A family could participate in an educational program. The volunteer opportunities need to be tailored to fit the needs of the particular family, which can involve considerable staff time to plan but can also be rewarding for both the families and the museum.

Corporate Volunteers

Communities with large industrial plants or corporations often encourage their employees to contribute volunteer hours to civic organizations. The companies may have human relations departments that help place employees in appropriate volunteer slots. Some corporations will also match volunteer hours with a cash contribution.

Distance Volunteers

With the growth of Internet use, there are opportunities for volunteers to support museums in new ways and in their own time. This opens new opportunities for volunteers who are employed. They can do research from home. They might be able to enter data about collections. They could develop educational materials that correlate with state-mandated educational goals.

Community Service Volunteers

Some museums have found that with the right supervision, individuals who have been sentenced to public service after breaking the law may be able to lend support to museums. Each museum needs to weigh the potential for their assistance with possible security risks.[4]

Information Technology Support

As technological changes sweep our society, some museums are on the wrong side of the digital divide. With limited budgets and often outdated equipment, such museums can benefit greatly from savvy volunteers who know how to use technology to the museum's advantage and where to look for assistance in upgrading the museum's skills and equipment. People with technological skills can also help the museum with a website and with social networking through venues such as Facebook, Twitter, and Flickr. As with all volunteers, it is important to have clearly established objectives and responsibilities in writing for both the information technology volunteer and the museum.[5]

Steps in Developing a Viable Volunteer Program

It would be wonderful to have a corps of museum volunteers willing to assist with every possible task at any possible moment. But people have numerous demands on their time. Many families include two adults who work full-time. How can a museum compete? There is no easy answer and certainly no single solution, but there are ways to develop a successful volunteer program.

Recruitment

Some museums are very successful in recruiting enthusiastic volunteers. How do they do it? One approach is to start with the volunteer instead of the museum. Rather than concentrating on the museum's need for volunteers, one might look at the demographics of a locale, identify potential volunteers, and assess what a museum has that might attract them. Who is the audience for the museum? Does the current volunteer pool reflect the makeup of the community? What about the exhibits and programs of the museum? If volunteers do not see themselves in the overall programs of the museum, they are not likely to want to participate. A museum that makes a commitment to serve its entire community needs to take steps to ensure that its volunteer corps reflects the diversity of its public. This is a long-term goal that requires support from the board and all staff members.

What other organizations are active in the community? What might the museum offer that is different? Perhaps the museum has (or could have) evening hours to attract volunteers who work during the day. Maybe it could offer a family-oriented volunteer opportunity, which might appeal to grandparents or single parents. Maybe someone could work from home on a computer. Of course, it is always important to keep the museum's purpose and mission in mind. How might volunteers become involved in supporting the mission? It is sometimes overlooked that establishing and maintaining viable volunteer programs entails costs in time and money. Expenses for office space, supplies, printing, and mailing need to be considered and budgeted for, even in all-volunteer organizations.[6]

The best method of recruitment is through current volunteers. Sometimes a happy volunteer is willing to bring a friend to a museum event or to an open house for potential volunteers. A person who has never been to the museum might be more likely to come with someone he or she knows. Some people will get interested in a particular program or exhibit that needs extra help, then stay to help with something else. Some individuals are interested strictly in special events. They immerse themselves wholeheartedly for a limited period, then back off for a while. This is often true of people who may spend part of the year in another locale.

There are as many different kinds of volunteers as there are needs for services. The trick is to match them up. Some of the top reasons people give for volunteering include helping others, having clearly defined responsibilities, doing interesting work, admiring the competence of the immediate supervisor, and receiving supervisor guidance.[7] Social motivations should not be overlooked. Volunteers enjoy meeting new people and working with them on projects in which they have a mutual interest. Even stuffing envelopes can be fun when done with people one enjoys being around. Often people volunteer because they want to make a difference. It is good to keep in mind that one of the main reasons people give for not volunteering is that they have not been asked.

Volunteers can be recruited through a notice in the museum's newsletter, on its website, or in the local newspaper. National websites, such as Volunteer Match.com, link volunteers with nonprofits, and some states now have similar statewide networks. Museum sites, however, are not always listed. Museum members are an obvious source for potential volunteers, since they have already indicated an interest in the institution. Undergraduate and graduate students may find the museum an attractive place to gain work experience and possibly see if there might be a career fit. University job placement offices may be helpful here. Middle and high school students are also valuable volunteers, either individually or on group projects. A community volunteer center might assist in matching volunteers and nonprofit organizations. For a short project that needs some manpower, fraternal organizations or Scout groups might be interested. For a special project, such as a traveling exhibit that needs extra docents, it might be possible to spread the word through other civic organizations, teacher's organizations, the American Association of Retired People, or the Retired Senior Volunteer Program.

Volunteers should complete a job application before being accepted into a program. Textbox 3.1 summarizes areas to consider asking about in a volunteer application. There are numerous examples online. One rule of thumb is to seek

VOLUNTEER APPLICATION

The following summary is adapted from the Oberlin Heritage Center volunteer application form, a five-page document. The complete form is available on the museum's website (www.oberlinheritage.org/getinvolved/volunteer).

In addition to basic contact information, the museum uses the opportunity to obtain some background information on the volunteers, to learn about their skills and interests, and to determine where they might be placed. By including permission for the volunteer to be photographed, the museum avoids any problems later if the volunteer is included in publicity shots or other photos. The form alerts potential volunteers to background checks and the need to reveal any problems with the law. There is a special section for parents of youth volunteers to complete. Each museum should craft an application that meets its individual needs. Volunteer applications may be accompanied by job descriptions tailored to fit specific volunteer opportunities.

Application Form Areas
- *Personal information:* name, address, phone; preferred means of contact; permission to contact by mail or e-mail; status (employed, retired, student); employer or school; birth date (if under eighteen)
- *Emergency contact:* name, relationship, work phone, home phone, cell phone
- *Availability chart:* hours per week or month; special events; for students, length of volunteer commitment
- *Special skills, interests, previous experience:* working or volunteering in a museum
- *References:* two unrelated people who know of volunteer experience
- *Placement choices:* buildings and grounds, education and programming, oral history, open houses or tours, community improvement projects, collections, office, fundraising, etc.
- *Preferred place of work:* home, with others, alone
- *Reason for volunteering*
- *Additional comments*
- *Background checks and related information:* nondiscriminatory clause, possible background check, information regarding pending or previous civil or criminal actions, dismissal from any other volunteer program
- *Signed agreement:* no compensation, permission to be photographed, verification of information, compliance with rules and regulations
- *Special section for guardians of volunteers under the age of eighteen*

out models from museums accredited by the American Association of Museums (AAM). All of their policies and forms will have undergone scrutiny.[8] Typically, job descriptions will cover objectives, responsibilities, qualifications, time commitments, training, and evaluations, but any forms or policies should be adapted to fit a particular museum.[9] (See textbox 2.2 in chapter 2 of this book for a sample volunteer job description.) Often, potential volunteers complete an interview, which can help ensure the fit is right for the volunteer and the task. This may be confirmed by a written volunteer agreement that outlines the museum's expectations. It is crucial that the museum defines its expectations prior to seeking volunteer support. Lining up willing and enthusiastic volunteers and then having an inadequately planned opportunity for volunteering will quickly dry up volunteer resources and give the museum a poor reputation.

The recruitment period is also a time to complete background checks on potential volunteers and to obtain references. Anyone who will be working with children or handling money should automatically be screened in some way. People handling sums of money are commonly bonded. The museum's responsibility is to establish conditions that protect its assets. Sadly, insider thefts by trusted volunteers are not uncommon in museums, libraries, and other nonprofits.[10] Another unfortunate fact is that a very high percentage of sexual predators that infiltrate youth-serving organizations have no criminal history and maintain "trophy testimonials" to offer as references.[11] If a background check is considered advisable, the local police department can help. There are also online resources for background checks available for a small fee, and a registered sex offender list provides information about where known sex offenders live and work. Court records are also available online by county.

Checking local references and holding interviews with prospective volunteers can help to determine if a volunteer is appropriate for the museum. Some organizations obtain references but do not take time to follow up on them.

Orientation

All new volunteers should take part in a general orientation that acquaints them with the museum and its history, mission, vision, core values, and code of ethics. This is a good time to reinforce the benefits of volunteering—for the museum and for the volunteer. The volunteer manual will come in handy for the orientation of new volunteers. Some museums require their volunteers to sign an acknowledgment verifying that they have read the manual. This could be a part of the museum's risk management and insurance requirements. Orientation should include an in-person introductory meeting to go over logistics and amenities. Many aspects of a museum that have become familiar to longtime staff or volunteers may be new to an incoming volunteer. Newcomers may not know how to get into the building, where to put their belongings, or who has keys and access to parts of the building. For instance, museum storage areas should be locked, and there may be a sign-in sheet or a requirement for a staff person's presence to enter certain areas. This is true even in very small museums. Some aspects of the orientation can be covered by e-mails or materials mailed to new volunteers prior to their first visit. Some information might be posted in a section of the museum's website reserved for volunteers. These measures can save time and make the new recruits feel comfortable with the museum when they arrive.

Orientation will vary with the types of tasks volunteers will perform. Board members should have their own manual and orientation. Volunteers recruited for individual jobs will likely have a supervisor. Docents may be accepted in classes and may interact with, or have mentors from, earlier docent classes. Orientation may include a behind-the-scenes tour of the museum. It is essential to include a time for questions.

The point of orientation is to make new volunteers feel at home and a part of the museum. They need to feel they are accepted by the staff and board. This is the first test point for retaining new recruits. Volunteers who are confused or feel uncomfortable for some reason may bail out before they have gotten started, so planning and a good welcome are important in getting them settled in.

Training

The kind of volunteer task will determine the training offered. Some training may be individualized, such as teaching a volunteer how to enter data by using collections software. Other training may be geared for a group. Training to become a docent could involve several group sessions and perhaps outside reading. A new docent may be shadowed by an experienced one who can offer tips on giving an effective tour, or a new docent might follow along with a seasoned guide's tour. At the end of a training program, some museums test for knowledge and skills acquired.

Sometimes new volunteers have mentors who give them individual attention. A volunteer who moves into a special events slot might serve an apprenticeship with someone who has experience with a particular fundraising event. Written materials accumulated in various areas of operation may be a part of the training. For instance, a longtime fundraiser may have prepared extensive notes on time lines, committee structure, previous expenditures, attendance, and more that will help new special events volunteers get acclimated. Using experienced volunteers to assist in training new ones is beneficial for both the museum and the volunteers.[12]

All volunteers should have some training related to museum accessibility, even if they do not work directly with the public. Museums open to the public are required to be accessible to people with disabilities. A broad approach is to consider how accessible the museum is to all visitors, including seniors, parents with small children, and people for whom English is a second language (see chapter 4 in Book 4 of this series). Volunteers who serve as docents must be sensitive to visitors' many needs in order to help facilitate their museum experience. Volunteers who ordinarily work behind the scenes might be called into service during an emergency to help evacuate people with disabilities. Volunteers who work with collections might help identify objects that could be handled by blind visitors. Integrating accessibility into the museum's programs is part of understanding its mission, vision, and core values. A volunteer program needs to be part of a holistic approach to serving the public. It should be remembered that a museum accessible to visitors is also a place where people with disabilities can serve in many capacities as volunteers.

Feedback from volunteers indicates that one of the principal reasons people volunteer is to learn something new. Knowing that this is a motivation can suggest some ways to offer fresh learning opportunities. Training is provided to the new volunteer but should be ongoing. It can take the form of reading and discussion about current issues in museums or involve a visit to another museum. The concept of lifelong learning is a core value in museums and applies not only to visitors but also to volunteers (see the section on professional development in chapter 2 of this book).

Whatever the training, it should incorporate supervision and checkpoints. Maintaining good, two-way communication with volunteers is essential. This is a key area in which the museum develops the bond that will encourage the volunteer to buy into the museum's programs and become a working part of the team. When communication breaks down, volunteers can drift off and lose interest. Communication may be written, given in person or through e-mail, posted on a bulletin board, or perhaps published in a special newsletter for volunteers. Information may be sent to all volunteers, but each volunteer needs also to have one-on-one contact with someone.

Recognition

Part of communicating with volunteers involves recognizing their contributions. This cannot be stressed enough. Knowing what the volunteers have contributed is basic to recognition. Tracking volunteer time can be accomplished by requiring them to sign in and record their hours. A simple notebook can be used for them to enter their names, date of service, role, and number of hours. Tallying the records monthly keeps everything up to date, and these figures can be used for monthly board reports. The record of volunteer hours can be used in support of grant requests, in fundraising, and in other applications.

Recognition may take the form of a simple thank-you, or it may be as elaborate as a dinner with awards. The key is that it be a genuine expression of thanks for the efforts of the volunteer. Recognition may be tangible or intangible. In this area, it is especially helpful to exchange ideas with museum colleagues. Networking with other museums through workshops and conferences might uncover new ideas for recognizing volunteers, such as featuring profiles of volunteers in the museum's newsletter or on its website, providing honorary parking spaces, posting volunteers' pictures in the museum, holding annual lunches or dinners, awarding prizes, sending postcards and notes, acknowledging birthdays or other anniversaries, making a gift of a book for the museum library in the volunteer's name, sending a letter to a school or employer that acknowledges the volunteer's contribution, or celebrating National Volunteer Week in April. The kinds of recognition vary with the kinds of volunteers. If the museum is actively seeking volunteers from new sources, it will need to be innovative in choosing an appropriate kind of recognition for them. The typical award dinner may not suit all situations.

Some organizations plan outings for volunteers. These might be combined with training opportunities. For instance, collections volunteers might find it interesting to tour behind the scenes at a nearby museum to see how it deals with storage and other issues. Docents might enjoy attending a special exhibit. All of the museum's volunteers might have fun visiting the opening of a new museum together.

At some point, a museum may need to face the death of an active volunteer. This is an extremely individual situation, and it may be helpful to consult with colleagues who have faced similar circumstances. Depending on the family's wishes, it may be appropriate to send cards or flowers. Some museums have initiated special memorial funds; others have purchased a book with a memorial plate, planted a tree in the volunteer's name, written about the volunteer in the museum newsletter, or recognized a service that was close to the volunteer. The aim is to acknowledge the difference that the volunteer made in the museum.[13]

Evaluation

Volunteer evaluation is sometimes neglected. Supervisors may hesitate to evaluate volunteers because the museum needs their help; the volunteers are contributing their time, and it is sometimes feared that, if offended, they might depart. However, as with other areas of museum operation, if a professional attitude is maintained, it usually will be respected. A good approach is to use self-evaluation. This gives volunteers the chance to examine their own performance and to evaluate the museum's program. The volunteers can compare their expectations with those of the museum as expressed in the job description, and they can offer valuable feedback to the museum. The individual volunteer's evaluation can also become a part of an evaluation of the entire volunteer program, which should be undertaken periodically.

Legal and Ethical Concerns

The museum has oversight responsibilities of for all people who visit or work there, for the museum's finances, and for the museum's physical resources, including the collections. The museum must maintain a safe environment for volunteers, staff, and visitors. This is achieved in part via written guides, including job descriptions, codes of ethics, policies, and procedures. These help the volunteer to know what behavior is expected and what is not appropriate. It is the museum's responsibility to be aware of legislation that may affect volunteer participation. Under the Volunteer Protection Act (VPA), which became a federal law in 1997, volunteers serving nonprofit organizations are not liable for harm caused by an act or omission, although state regulations cover exceptions and circumstances. The VPA defines a volunteer as "an individual performing services for a nonprofit organization or a governmental entity who does not receive: A) compensation (other than reasonable reimbursement for expenses actually incurred); or B) any other thing of value in lieu of compensation, in excess of $500 per year, and such term includes a volunteer serving as a director, officer, trustee, or direct service volunteer."[14] In addition, although a volunteer may be covered by the VPA or state legislation, the museum will still be held liable for negligence caused by volunteers. Therefore, museums must be conscientious about defining the scope of volunteers' responsibilities. Volunteers acting outside the scope of their job descriptions may not be covered by the VPA. Volunteers also need to be aware of how provisions of the museum's code of ethics affect them.

A museum's volunteer program should be built into the institution's overall risk management guidelines. This involves identifying risks and devising ways to mitigate them. A list of risk management tools that should be included in all volunteer programs can be found in a useful volume titled *Transforming Museum Volunteering: A Practical Guide for Engaging 21st Century Volunteers.*[15] Liability issues that concern volunteers should be considered as a component of the museum's insurance. The museum's insurance rates may be affected by some volunteer roles, such as those involving use of power equipment in constructing exhibits, driving vehicles for museum business, climbing ladders, or handling money. Volunteers may be included as additional insureds or could have their own policies. Some states recognize the right to workers' compensation for volunteers (see chapter 4 of Book 2 of this series).

As noted in the above discussion on recruitment, there are special requirements for volunteers who will be working with children. It is vital to maintain the museum's reputation as a safe haven. Once that reputation is damaged, it is hard to regain. Volunteers always need to put the well-being of the museum first and avoid the appearance of a conflict of interest. Some museums ask volunteers to sign a disclosure form that lists areas of personal or professional interest that might present a problem. These might include gifts or favors for the museum volunteer or close family, violations of museum confidentiality, or use of museum property for personal business.[16]

Firing or Retiring a Volunteer

Despite the saying "You can't fire a volunteer," sometimes it is necessary to do so for the well-being of the museum and those who work in and visit it. There is no point in establishing guidelines and codes of conduct if they are not followed. Ignoring these guidelines sends a message that behavior outside the rules will be tolerated. The thoughtful recruitment, orientation, training, and evaluation of volunteers and the use of written tools such as job descriptions, placement agreements, and volunteer manuals all help to avoid problems and will provide a foundation for action if it becomes necessary. In *Transforming Museum Volunteering*, dismissal is said usually to be due to problems of performance or conduct, and several practical steps are outlined that can help the museum confront this difficult situation.[17]

A related problem may occur when it comes time to retire a long-standing volunteer who is no longer able to provide the level of service he or she once could. Sometimes a less demanding role can be found for the volunteer. A person who can no longer carry out the strenuous tasks of the docent may be able to help at a reception desk or with interviewing for an oral history project. But the volunteer may no longer be capable of participating at all. There is no easy way to meet this situation. The goal is to retire the volunteer with grace and dignity through some kind of recognition. This will vary according to the volunteer. In such a situation, comparing notes with colleagues might help one find the appropriate gesture. Many museums encounter this dilemma—one better dealt with sooner rather than later.

Auxiliary Groups

Many museums have supporting auxiliary organizations. These groups may be loosely organized as advisory committees, as friends groups under the umbrella of the museum's governing structure, or as full-blown auxiliary organizations with constitutions, bylaws, and tax-exempt status. There are many positive aspects to having groups of museum supporters organized to provide services to further the museum's mission. An auxiliary can relieve staff of administrative issues, such as tracking volunteer hours; assist in recruiting volunteers for needed positions; and act as a respected partner in initiating new programs.

Conflict sometimes arises, however, if the degree of autonomy of the auxiliary is unclear. Sometimes auxiliaries raise funds for a special project, then learn the museum neither needs nor desires it. Auxiliaries can overstep their roles in managing volunteer programs. Most of these issues can be avoided by some planning and communication. Advice from the museum's legal counsel on fundraising, paid personnel, serving alcohol, and sales could avoid problems.[18]

A museum contemplating forming an auxiliary group could gain insight by looking at some established museum auxiliary groups and perhaps talking to both auxiliary leaders and museum staff about how the program works and any pitfalls to avoid. It would be essential to have a written agreement stating the auxiliary's goals and establishing guidelines for reporting and accounting.[19] Creating and maintaining good communication between the museum's governing body and staff and the auxiliary would also set up a climate for a successful partnership.

Who's in Charge?

Museums are very dependent on the support of volunteers, some entirely so. Museums are best served by volunteer programs with some structure and organization, but this requires a considerable investment of time. The responsibilities for operating such a program are typically assigned to a coordinator or manager of volunteers. This is frequently a paid position, but in a small museum, a volunteer might fill this slot. A volunteer willing to undertake this role will find it both rewarding and challenging. Many resources can help—in person, in print, and online. Opportunities for professional development are offered through workshops and conferences. Written policies, job descriptions, and a volunteer handbook will provide a solid foundation that will make the volunteer manager's tasks much easier. Creating a defined process for volunteers to undergo, from recruitment to evaluation, will offer a clear path. These are important tools for even the smallest museums, and they can protect the museum from liability. Museums with strong volunteer programs have found that in a time of need, when outside funding is threatened, volunteers often take a leadership role in demonstrating how museums serve their communities. Such support can make a difference for the future of museums.

Resources

Many resources can help a small museum build a volunteer program. Membership in the American Association for Museum Volunteers (AAMV) would be a start. This organization is the only national association representing more than a million volunteers in all categories of museums. The AAMV is affiliated with the American Association of Museums (AAM) and with the World Federation of Friends of Museums. It promotes professional standards of volunteerism; offers workshops and panels at state, regional, national, and international meetings; hosts an e-mail list for AAMV members; produces publications; and advocates for museums. The membership fee is modest for the benefits received.

A useful publication issued by the AAMV in 2007 is *Transforming Museum Volunteering: A Practical Guide for Engaging 21st Century Volunteers*. This handy paperback (cited in note 15 of this chapter) is full of good advice that is applicable to small museums, and it contains numerous forms, sample policies, and evaluation guidelines. It has an excellent section on resources that includes an annotated bibliography. This book can be purchased directly from AAMV or from the AAM bookstore.

Museums that have developed good job descriptions, policies, and procedures are often willing to share them. Several museums with admirable volunteer manuals are willing to make them available as models. They include the Chester County Historical Society, West Chester, Pennsylvania; the McLean County Museum of History, Bloomington, Illinois; the DuPage Children's Museum, Naperville, Illinois; and the Missouri History Museum, St. Louis, Missouri. These museums are not small themselves, but their handbooks cover topics applicable to small museums. While these handbooks are good models, they should be tailored to fit the needs of specific museums.

Many online resources deal with volunteerism. Do not look only for museum examples. Volunteer programs in other nonprofit organizations will offer many creative and useful ideas.

State and regional museum service organizations have many resources for small museums. They offer workshops and other training that may address volunteerism. They may provide field services through telephone, e-mail, and on-site consultations. Some have circulating libraries that contain information about volunteers. They can often put you directly in contact with a source that will have just the right answer for a question.

Online Resources

There are several helpful online resources. All of those given below were accessed on June 30, 2010.

Charity Channel (www.charitychannel.com): The website for Charity Channel offers many different articles and forums for discussion of topics related to nonprofit organizations. *Volunteer Management Review* is a free, biweekly feature devoted to volunteerism. Click on "Articles" and scroll down to "Volunteer Management Review."

Energize, Inc. (www.energizeinc.com): This website includes useful articles, a free monthly newsletter, and an online journal edited by Susan Ellis.

Independent Sector (www.independentsector.org): This nationally recognized organization advocates for nonprofits and maintains the Giving and Volunteering Research Clearinghouse, with information about volunteerism.

Merrill Associates Topic of the Month (www.merrillassociates.com): This site contains short articles about many current volunteer-related topics.

Several e-mail lists address issues related to volunteering: Museum-Ed (www.museum-ed.org) grew out of EdCom, a standing professional committee of the AAM. Museum-Ed is a nonprofit organization dedicated to providing museum educators opportunities to ask questions, exchange ideas, explore current issues, share resources, reflect on experiences, and inspire new directions in museum education. Museum-Ed is not a membership organization. All of the resources on the Museum-Ed website are free and available to educators in any type of museum, as well as to anyone interested in the field of museum education. Another e-mail list, Museum-L (http://home.ease.lsoft.com/archives/museum-l.html), covers general museum issues, but it sometimes addresses volunteerism. One may subscribe to the e-mail list or access discussions through the site's archives.

Acknowledgments

Several colleagues generously shared information about working with volunteers. They include Mary Anne Shierman, McLean County Museum of History, Bloomington, Illinois; Natasha Johnson, Missouri History Museum, St. Louis, Missouri; Shelly Hanover, Children's Discovery Museum, Normal, Illinois; Diane Ernst, DuPage Children's Museum, Naperville, Illinois; Shannon Reedy, Miller Park Zoo, Bloomington, Illinois; Patricia Murphy, Oberlin Heritage Center, Oberlin, Ohio; and Ellen Endslow, Chester County Historical Society, West Chester, Pennsylvania. I am grateful to Illinois Heritage Association editor Carol Betts for many helpful suggestions.

Notes

1. Joan Kuyper with Ellen Cochran Hirzy and Kathleen Huftalen, *Volunteer Program Administration: A Handbook for Museums and Other Cultural Institutions* (New York: American Council for the Arts, 1993), 62.

2. Many states have organizations such as Volunteer Lawyers for the Arts and CPAs for the Public Interest, which may be able to suggest potential trustees or advisors. These organizations can usually be accessed online.

3. Patricia L. Miller, *Volunteerism: Gifts of Time and Talent*, Part 1, Illinois Heritage Association (IHA) Technical Insert 113 (Champaign, IL: IHA, 2001), 4.

4. Miller, *Volunteerism*, Part 1, 3.

5. Miller, *Volunteerism*, Part 1.

6. Kuyper et al., *Volunteer Program Administration*, 17.

7. Kuyper et al., *Volunteer Program Administration*, 46.

8. Examples include the Japanese American National Museum, Los Angeles, California; Calvert Marine Museum, Solomons, Maryland; and McLean County Museum of History, Bloomington, Illinois. The British Museum has a short, useful policy on volunteering, available online at www.britishmuseum.org/PDF/Volunteering.pdf (accessed December 24, 2009).

9. Kuyper et al., *Volunteer Program Administration*, 38.

10. Patricia L. Miller, *Volunteerism*, Part 2, 2.

11. David Allburn, "Screening for Sexual Predators," January 2001, www.merrill associates.com/topic/2005/01/screening-sexual-predators (accessed December 24, 2009).

12. Miller, *Volunteerism*, Part 2, 2.

13. Miller, *Volunteerism*, Part 2, 3.

14. "Volunteer Protection Act of 1997," Nebraska Department of Insurance, www.doi .ne.gov/shiip/volunteer/pl_105.19.pdf (accessed December 24, 2009).

15. Ellen Hirzy, for the American Association for Museum Volunteers, *Transforming Museum Volunteering: A Practical Guide for Engaging 21st Century Volunteers* (Bloomington, IN: AuthorHouse), 66.

16. Kuyper et al., *Volunteer Program Administration*, 19.

17. Hirzy, *Transforming Museum Volunteering*, 61–62.

18. Kuyper et al., *Volunteer Program Administration*, 18.

19. Miller, *Volunteerism*, Part 1, 2.

CHAPTER FOUR
LET'S GET AN INTERN: MANAGING A SUCCESSFUL INTERNSHIP PROGRAM
Amanda Wesselmann

Th is chapter on internships provides a template for history museums and cultural organizations to begin a successful internship program that will benefit both the organization and the interns. Internship programs can be daunting to start or revamp, and this chapter presents a step-by-step approach that will benefit museums at all stages of internship program development or retooling. First, the chapter defines internships and discusses some of the characteristics of interns; it then outlines the steps for recruiting interns and finally lays a foundation for managing them effectively.

What Is an Internship?

An internship is generally considered to be an agreement between a student and an organization in which the student works for the organization in exchange for educational experience and skill development opportunities. Internships can be paid or unpaid. They are most often for a set period, such as a number of hours, but they can last for the duration of a specific project. An internship is not, however, free labor from young people who should be grateful for any experience they get. An educational experience is paramount to the internship, and ideal internships combine daily operations with a project. Museums should not bring interns on board with the sole intent to have an extra pair of hands to perform mundane tasks regular staff do not want to do. There are many ways to structure an internship, of course, and in the end the best internships are those that benefit both the organization and the intern.

Compensation

The currency of internships varies by the organization and availability of resources. Large businesses can often offer paid internships; nonprofit organizations are rarely so lucky as to have the amount of discretionary funding that stipends require, but creativity can solve that problem. At times, grants can be obtained for project-specific interns. Few grants will pay for general operating support, however, so interns must be working on a goal-oriented project rather than answering the phone while the staff works on a project. Possible sources for this type of grant include local community foundations, state humanities and arts councils, and the federal Institute of Museum and Library Services. Private foundations provide other options if projects dovetail with the foundation's interests. Grants are usually awarded as a lump sum, covering the cost of paying the intern as well as materials and other aspects of the project. Interns do not usually expect or receive fringe benefits such as health insurance or overtime pay due to the transitory nature of their employment. Payment can be made on whatever schedule suits the intern, organization, and any applicable grant requirements. The Noble County Historical Society, an all-volunteer organization in Albion, Indiana, obtained grants to pay interns an hourly wage and tracked intern work with time cards.

In other cases, the tangible reward for the student is course credit or another check on their list of academic requirements. These are often called "unpaid internships," but the student is compensated with course credit. Credit is usually negotiated with the university or college so that the student receives a number of credit hours commensurate with the amount of time spent working for the organization, such as three credit hours for nine hours per week at the museum. Often, credit-based internship requirements include a reflection paper from the student about the internship, as well as an evaluation or other review of the student's performance from the museum.

Some internships are truly unpaid. Due to a variety of factors, such as having to pay to enroll in credit hours or the unavailability of faculty advisors during the summer, some interns are willing to work for free. This has been the case at both the Morris-Butler House Museum in Indianapolis, Indiana, and the General Lew Wallace Study & Museum in Crawfordsville, Indiana. At both institutions the students receive the same project orientation, supervision, and evaluation of a typical internship even though the interns are not compensated. These interns are rare, but they can be among the most motivated because the experience is all they receive.

Characteristics of Interns

Most, but not all, interns are students pursuing either graduate or undergraduate degrees. Some are recent graduates who want or need the experience before pursuing a full-time career in a history organization. Whether or not they are students, however, interns share a number of characteristics. All interns want real experience, have or are obtaining academic training related to the internships they seek, and want to make a difference in the field. Looking at the following three different groups of interns—undergraduate students, graduate students, and recent graduates—can help one know what to expect from each type.

Undergraduate Students

Undergraduate students are often completing requirements for their academic programs and may view an internship as similar to a required class. To many undergrads, an internship is an opportunity to get out in the world and learn something new. They will eagerly do most things they are asked, come from the most technology-literate generation, and can excel at computer-related tasks. What they have in enthusiasm, though, they may lack in work experience. Undergrads require the most supervision and are often the least disciplined in terms of self-motivation. These students' employment history often consists of stereotypical summer jobs outside the traditional business environment, and they will require instruction in the expectations for dress, conduct, and workplace etiquette at your institution. They may need a fast pace to keep interested, which supervisors can provide by setting deadlines, checking in often, and assigning a range of tasks.

Photo 4.1. Undergraduate students are often eager to try different tasks, but they require close supervision from staff.

Graduate Students

Graduate students are also often completing requirements for a master's or doctoral program, but they are motivated to gain real-world experience and make use of the knowledge they have newly acquired from their coursework. Graduate students can often motivate themselves and are more experienced with working in different settings, but they still require explanations of workplace etiquette standards. Their additional life experience, coursework, and more definite career trajectory give them the knowledge, skills, and enthusiasm to tackle jobs that may be too complex or specialized for undergraduate students. Graduate students are often excited about completing projects, and one of the challenges is helping them negotiate the balance between time and quality. For instance, collections work requires describing artifacts, but taking two days to measure and write a description for one object is likely not the best use of time.

Recent Graduates

Recent graduates of both bachelor's and master's programs are similar to graduate students but perhaps even more eager to gain experience, get a foot in the door to find employment, and possibly see if they want to pursue a career in museums. Paid internships are the greatest draw for these interns as they no longer need credit for a program and are often looking for a way to make money while building experience in their newly chosen field. Often, though, they will take an unpaid intern position if it will give them experience they need and they can still meet all their expenses. Recent graduates can have challenging schedules in that they usually have other jobs they are balancing at the same time.

Know What to Expect

In general, interns are excited to work in a real business, eager to tackle their projects, and ready to learn new things. They are often surprised by how much they learn. While supervising volunteers and interns can be similar, there are different sets of expectations for these two groups. Volunteers usually come in for regular shifts or special events on an ongoing basis. They often have a variety of motivations, such as helping the community, meeting different people, and using their skills in a new way. By contrast, most internships are project based. Interns come for a set amount of time to complete a requirement, earn course credit or a stipend, and gain valuable real-world experience. Volunteers have often been in the workforce for an extended period, while this is often the first time interns have worked outside the classroom or a summer job. As students, interns are inherently in a state of transition that can require more supervision for a quality product. And while you would expect volunteers to know how to dress appropriately, conduct themselves properly in a business setting, and even clean up after their breaks, interns still need education in these areas.

While workplace etiquette may seem like something students should have learned from their parents, teachers, and previous employers, this is often not the case. Moreover, family life and classrooms are not professional companies, and lessons attempted there may not actually take root in students until they see their application in an actual business setting. One college internship coordinator recounted a conversation with a student's mother who wanted internships to emphasize those lessons of courtesy and dressing appropriately because whenever the parents said something, the student just rolled her eyes and dismissed their comments. This is an essential part of supervising interns, whether it is continuing these students' education in life skills or training the next generations of professionals. It is an area where interns' judgment is often inadequate, and many students believe they know the ropes when in fact they are laboring under misconceptions. Even phrases that supervisors often think are clear can be misconstrued: "Business casual dress" means khakis and a polo shirt to some but jeans and a T-shirt without holes to others, so giving the example of khakis and a polo shirt will define the phrase. You can expect interns to learn quickly, but expecting them to come into your organization with full knowledge of how to act and work in this new environment sets both the organization and the intern up to fail. The final sections of this chapter outline some areas to cover in training and supervising interns.

Benefits of Internships

A well-run internship program can and should be mutually beneficial. Students gain credit or a stipend and valuable real-world experience. The organization, in turn, gains labor, partnerships with educational institutions, an increased reputation as an educational organization, and the advantage of instructing the next generations of professionals.

Benefits to the Interns

Interns are compensated either with a stipend or credits, but the experience they receive is far more valuable and longer lasting than immediate payment. The classroom setting of most colleges affords a learning-intensive environment for many people, but actual experience is something that cannot be gained from a lecture. Managing projects, working with others, multitasking, and conducting oneself in a businesslike manner are all areas where a good internship provides instruction and opportunity to develop skills. Will Finney, intern for the General Lew Wallace Study & Museum for two academic years, returned for his second internship to create a new orientation video because "it has provided an opportunity to pursue my love of film." The museum, in turn, balanced its needs by serving visitors better with an updated video.

Benefits to the Organization

One of the greatest and most obvious benefits of an internship program for a museum is the contributions that interns make to the overall efforts of the institution. Interns, even paid ones, are less expensive than staff. They are almost always willing to try new things, and dedicated interns will devote themselves to producing quality products. According to Dr. Michael William Doyle, associate professor of history at Ball State University in Muncie, Indiana, smaller organizations can sometimes gain the most: "We had a student who wanted to work with the local historical society in his hometown. They hadn't really hosted interns before, but the work he did with their photograph collection helped the organization immensely." Writing job descriptions can help the museum internally by requiring staff to break up work into discreet projects, thereby making the work more manageable and employing student help in the process of completing goals.

Providing opportunities for students to gain real-world experience in the careers that a degree program is preparing them for opens a door to collaboration with traditional educational institutions. Four- and two-year colleges in particular can provide museums with a workforce while meeting their goals of educating students. As the partnership grows, the two institutions can work together to match the needs of the programs and the nature of the work that needs to be completed.

Additionally, museums can build their reputations as educational institutions. The more you have to offer students, including work-based educational opportunities like internships, the more you solidify the organization's reputation in the community as an educational resource. College staff and student interns are good publicists, and the projects completed by interns can build good news coverage in the community about how you are thinking outside the box to educate people. A solid internship program is one way to demonstrate that museums are not just for elementary school students anymore.

Today's interns are the adults who will visit museums in the next five to ten years. Students will carry a good internship experience with them for years, which can help foster goodwill and understanding between museums and the public. Moreover, few people have been "behind the scenes" at a museum, giving these organizations a certain mystique that interns can help dispel when they share their knowledge with their families and friends. This increase in understanding will help the public understand why it is important to behave in certain ways in museums and also why museums are valuable assets to the community. (See textbox 4.2 for more project ideas.)

Starting or Revamping an Internship Program

It is easy to say, "Let's get an intern," but internships require a framework that must be thoroughly thought through in order to be effective. Organizations need to identify work for the interns, contact colleges and universities, write effective job descriptions for the available projects, interview potential interns, and hire the final candidate. The process is similar to filling a regular, paid staff position, and the organization's current hiring process can serve as a framework for starting an internship program. After interns are hired, though, they require supervision and evaluation in ways that can be vastly different from paid staff.

Identifying Work

Before recruiting interns, museum staff need to assess what types of work need to be done in the coming months, as well as what groundwork needs to be laid, before sending out the word to recruit students. Because internships are supposed to be learning experiences for the students, they need to involve projects and aspects of organizations that will develop interns' skills and add to their body of knowledge while helping the museum. Ideally, intern assignments will be stand-alone projects that interns can complete within the prescribed time of the internship. When this is not possible, identify a phase or portion of a project so that the intern can complete something tangible and reach a good stopping point. For example, when the Noble County Historical Society wanted to digitize its collections records, it recruited interns to enter paper records into the computer database. On the other hand, it may be unrealistic to expect a summer intern to plan, execute, and wrap up the museum's biggest public program in the eight to ten weeks that summer internships normally span.

In addition to an overarching project, both organization and student often find it mutually beneficial if the internship also involves aspects of daily operations. Part of working for a small organization includes wearing many hats, and incorporating day-to-day activities into the internship increases the educational value for the student and benefits the organization. An intern's main project can be an aspect of daily operations, such as serving visitors, because the intern still gets the experience of working with the public and making history relevant to modern patrons. The key to including daily operations in an internship is conveying that information up front, ideally in both a written job description and the initial interview. The Morris-Butler House Museum, for instance, has acquired interns to conduct public tours, freeing time for the two full-time and one part-time staff members to perform other essential tasks.

Examine all aspects of the museum: Collections, education, exhibits, marketing, fundraising, and grounds work can open the possibilities for a well-

TEXTBOX 4.1

QUESTIONS TO CONSIDER ABOUT POTENTIAL INTERNSHIP PROJECTS

- Can a graduate or undergraduate student complete the task?
- How long an internship will be required for both training and task execution?
- What, if any, specialized knowledge is required?
- Does the museum have the staff and time to supervise the intern effectively?
- Does the project meet the museum's strategic goals?
- What skills does the intern need to have already in order to complete the project?
- What skills will the intern gain from this project?

fitting match with a student in a program that is not directly related to history. For instance, a student majoring in computer science could help a museum revamp its website. Sometimes previous interns will return with an additional project in mind. According to Aimee Rose Formo, project coordinator at Morris-Butler House Museum, several students have returned to finish projects or expand into a different area of museum operations. If possible, identify several projects and brainstorm all the possible academic links before contacting colleges and universities.

Contacting Colleges and Universities

Once you have identified one or more possible intern projects, contact area colleges and universities to investigate their requirements and ask about their system for internships. As most internships are for course credit or to fill another academic requirement, an established system often requires you to work through certain channels within the institution. Occasionally, colleges have funding for stipends for interns to cultural institutions. Other internship programs are far less structured and require students and professors to seek out opportunities. If your organization can provide a stipend through a grant or other funding source, then the college can be a great partner in spreading the word about the opportunity. This was the case at the Noble County Historical Society. With a project in mind and a grant to fund summer interns over two years, Margaret Ott, volunteer collections manager at the Noble County Historical Society,

TEXTBOX 4.2

INTERNSHIP PROJECTS

- Undertaking research projects, such as researching background information for an exhibit
- Inventorying collections
- Planning and executing a public program
- Marketing public programs
- Developing a website
- Securing supply or fund donations for specific projects
- Undertaking landscaping or grounds maintenance projects
- Developing a business plan for the gift shop
- Revamping or creating tours or educational programs
- Gathering benchmark information from other organizations
- Conducting a visitor study

Unlikely Internship Projects
- Acting as your office manager
- Serving as a routine maintenance person or gofer
- Conserving or treating collections
- Supervising volunteers
- Planning and executing a large fundraising event

called Ball State University and Indiana University, South Bend, to ask if they could publicize the available internships. As a result, the museum got two undergraduate students who helped enter collections data into a new database. Some colleges leave the details of compensation and paperwork to museum staff to sort out with the student. If possible, use an existing structure to your advantage and plug into its system. Either way, you need to connect with the right person to get the ball rolling.

Finding the right person takes a bit of research and some guessing on the part of museum staff. College websites and directories can often give information about how to find internships, and some even contain information for organizations that would like to provide internship opportunities. In some cases, the department for career services and job placements is the go-to place for internships. These departments often have specific guidelines for submitting internships and hiring interns. From 2005 through 2010, Wabash College in Crawfordsville, Indiana, used a grant to pay stipends for interns at cultural institutions; the grant facilitator was a wonderful resource for recruiting interns and developing the internship program. To make sure the grant, the college, the students, and the internship organizations were all satisfied, Wabash College set up a particular system in which a committee reviewed application materials for potential interns and passed along only the best applicants to the internship organizations. Then it was up to the cultural organization to interview and decide whether to hire from the final candidates.

Other institutions provide internships through specific academic departments, such as history, anthropology, education, fine arts, marketing, business, or other related fields. At these colleges, departmental secretaries are often instrumental in lining up the project with the internship standards there, as well as getting the word out to faculty and students. In places with graduate programs, especially those specifically in museum studies or a similar specialty, the graduate student coordinator of that program can be particularly helpful in building a partnership to get graduate students internship experience. At Indiana University–Purdue University Indianapolis (IUPUI), the museum studies graduate program has an e-mail distribution list that faculty and university staffers frequently use to send out information on job and internship opportunities.

In more student-directed programs, connecting with the right person is more challenging. Look for one or two professors who can serve as faculty contacts and encourage students to seek internships. At the very least, there may be an e-mail list or bulletin board where you can advertise available and upcoming internships to students, who can then work out the details of compensation with a faculty advisor. Sometimes it is possible to post a full job description, but if space is limited, such an advertisement should contain, at a minimum, a brief description of the work, the amount of time expected, compensation (if known), and contact information.

When you have identified the most likely person to ask about internships and are ready to make the call, what do you say? Introduce yourself and your organization, and indicate that you are interested in providing internship opportunities for the college or university's students. Inquire about the institution's established system for internships, including who is in charge, how students are compensated, and what the requirements are. This first call is made to gather information, and it will likely take several conversations to work out all the details and actually set up a partnership. Once an internship site is in the system, though, it is much easier to get interns. Ball State University's Public History Program requires an internship, and faculty have access to a list of previous internship sites that they can point out to students.

QUESTIONS FOR COLLEGE INTERNSHIP COORDINATORS

- How do students obtain internships for credit?
- Is there any funding through the college to pay for stipends for interns at cultural organizations?
- What are the requirements for students to complete an internship either for credit or college-sponsored stipend: evaluation, a journal or reflection from the intern, documentation of projects?
- How do students find out about available internships in the area?
- What materials do I need to submit to advertise internships through the college or department? When are materials due and to whom do I send them?
- If we do get an intern from your institution, what do we need to do vis-à-vis offering the internship, tracking hours, requesting payment (if it is through the college), and any changes in the student's project?

Writing Job Descriptions

Once you have identified what type of work students can do and checked with the area colleges to see what information they need, you can draft job descriptions for the internships. Include these areas: required skills and abilities, museum contact information and an applicable college contact, compensation and its source, description of the project, eligible majors, museum background and location, and application requirements, including deadlines for submission. Make the descriptions of skills and abilities as elementary and inclusive as you can so that potential interns get a realistic idea of what the job will require. Only put one project in each job description. There is flexibility after the intern starts for supervising staff to gauge abilities and interests firsthand and then adjust the scope of the internship and include portions of another project.

Make sure all aspects of the internship are included in the job description. A well-worded job description can include daily operations, such as serving visitors with guided tours, selling items from the gift shop, answering phones, or providing clerical assistance, like filing or mailing. In the end, whatever you put in the job description must be what the intern does; otherwise, the organization is not upholding its end of the bargain. For that reason, sections of the job description that cover the intern's responsibilities, skills, and abilities should contain input from—if it is not written entirely by—the staff member who will be supervising

Photo 4.2.   Some interns are better suited for greeting visitors, others excel at behind-the-scenes projects, and a few can do both.

the intern. Write as descriptively as possible; things that are obvious to you will not be clear to someone unfamiliar with your organization or new to museum work.

A hastily written job description might read something like this: "Museum internship available researching Abraham Lincoln for an upcoming exhibit. Good writing skills are required. If interested, call this number." This description sounds more like a classified ad and might do if space is truly limited. In such a case, consider putting a phone number or e-mail address for more information; the wording here makes it sound like a phone call is the entire application process. Lacking details, the ad may attract casual inquiries, but neither the organization nor the student has enough information to make an informed decision. What other requirements are there? Will the intern do

SAMPLE JOB DESCRIPTION

Compare these sample sections of an internship job description, adapted from the General Lew Wallace Study & Museum intern job description, with the classified ad version. This job description is much longer, but it is more thorough and provides essential information for potential interns. It also conveys that the museum is a professional organization, and only serious students should apply.

Positions Available
One collections researcher position, scheduled for 130 hours during each semester of the 2009–2010 academic year for a total of 260 hours. Intern is expected to complete ten hours per week in shifts of two or more hours during the museum's standard hours of operation: 9:00 a.m. to 5:00 p.m., Monday through Saturday, and 1:00 p.m. to 5:00 p.m., Sunday.

Description
Intern will be responsible for cataloging portions of the museum's collections. Proposed cataloging projects include the archival collection, postcard collection, photograph collection, or Civil War letter collection. Cataloging includes ensuring data integrity within the collections database, researching provenance, and adding annotated bibliographies to artifact records. In addition to the individual project, the intern will also contribute to the efforts of the small staff by assisting in the daily operation of the museum, including serving visitors with guided tours, answering phones and visitor questions, opening and closing the museum, running the cash register, setting up for events, and performing clerical duties as necessary.

Abilities
- Responsible, reliable, and dedicated to excellent job performance
- Sincere interest in learning and documenting history
- Ability to learn information quickly through a variety of media, including books, verbal instructions, and independent research
- Self-motivated
- Ability to work independently and as part of a team

Skills
- Good written and verbal communication skills
- Computer experience and familiarity with Microsoft Word, Excel, and databases

- Research and organization
- Attention to detail
- Creative problem solving and ability to use available resources
- Professional behavior and dress
- Customer service
- Students studying history or other applicable majors (see "Description") are encouraged to apply

Application Requirements
- Letter of interest
- Resume summarizing work and volunteer experience that meet the description, abilities, and skills requirements.
- Contact information for two references from previous work, volunteer, or class experience.

anything else? What skills are necessary for those other tasks? What evidence of good writing skills do you want to see before filling the position? What is the time line for the project? Answering these questions initially will save time and effort in the long run.

Interviewing Potential Interns

Whether the intern will receive a stipend or course credit, once the application materials are in, treat the hiring process as you would for a staff member. It may be tempting to enlist the first person who shows any interest, but the right person for the job is the best overall candidate: someone who possesses a base of necessary skills, is able to learn the rest, and will work well with the existing staff and volunteers. Sort through the applications, weed out any that are incomplete or otherwise do not meet your standards, and then consider those that make the cut for interviews. If possible, select two or three candidates to interview for the position.

The interview process is the beginning of the education process for interns; few, if any, have ever before had to interview for a position at a professional organization. Set up a time to meet, and expect the intern candidate to arrive on time, dressed appropriately, and prepared for the interview. The staff person who will be the main supervisor for the intern should participate in the interview. This gives the person in charge of the project a chance to assess candidates' abilities and match the personalities of staff and interns, which can make or break an experience for both the intern and organization. If it is not possible

Photo 4.3. Researching, designing, and fabricating an exhibit takes a variety of skills, and a thorough job description helped land the right intern to complete the Ben-Hur Legacy Gallery at the General Lew Wallace Study & Museum.

for the immediate supervisor to assist with the interview, clear criteria for what the project entails can help the staff person coordinating interns to hire the best person for the job.

In addition to asking the typical business interview questions about interests and experience, consider asking an optional fun question, such as "What is the last book you read that was not for class?" or "What are some of your other interests?" These types of questions can give you insight into the type of person you may be hiring and whether the student will fit with the organization.

In addition to learning more about the potential intern, share information about the organization so that candidates can make an informed decision about whether to accept the position if they get an offer. Describe the organization overall and include how the intern will fit into the larger picture. Provide a snapshot of how an average day flows and specific ways that the intern will assist with operations. Make it clear that small organizations like this one require everyone to wear multiple hats and that all the intern's time will not be spent on the project that may have attracted his or her initial attention. Finally, clarify expectations—an internship is a job, not a class that can be skipped at will. Interns are expected to arrive on time and ready to work, and if something like an illness comes up, then they are expected to call or e-mail their supervisors as soon as possible.

The last thing to do before making the final decision about hiring an intern is to contact references. Call after the interview, when you have an impression

---

TEXTBOX 4.5

SAMPLE INTERVIEW QUESTIONS FOR POTENTIAL INTERNS

- Why are you interested in this organization?
- What attracted you to this internship?
- How do you hope to benefit from an internship here at the museum?
- These are some of our goals. . . . How do you think your skills can help us meet these?
- What is your dream job?
- Have you ever volunteered before? What did you do?
- How do you learn things best? (This is especially important if you are responsible for hiring someone who will work with another staff person.)
- Describe a time when you had a difficult time completing a project. How did you handle it?

of the candidate, and ask, supervisor to supervisor, if the reference thinks the candidate has what it takes. Talking to someone who has worked closely with a candidate can help give a well-rounded picture after an interview, when students are likely on their best behavior.

Making the Offer

One of the questions from the initial series of conversations with the university or college covered the appropriate way to work with its system to offer a student an internship. Follow this process, checking with the appropriate person at the institution for clarification if needed. Often, there is no specific paperwork to submit for offering a candidate an internship, but even if the college does not require a formal offer letter, use that as a tool. One reason for doing so is that this is real-world practice for the student, and professional jobs mean official letters. The more pressing reason, though, is that having everything in writing is a safety measure for your organization and assures that all the parameters are set out in advance. Make three copies on letterhead: one for the student, one for the student's file at your organization, and one for the college. Even if the university does not require a copy, send one to the person coordinating internships. This conveys your expectations, especially if the intern does not work out as anticipated; it also communicates that your organization is professional.

The offer letter should include the parameters for the internship. Include the start and end dates, or the limits for setting up such a date if it has yet to be determined. Also include the nature of the internship and duties that the intern will perform, which can be paraphrased or copied-and-pasted from the job description. The offer letter should also cover the number of hours that the student will work, the nature of payment and how it will be received, and who will supervise the intern. Finally, list any other details that will be decided by e-mail or phone communications before the start of the internship. For instance, for an internship with a flexible schedule, the organization and the intern can determine a workweek that suits both parties between the making of the offer and the start date.

Consider making the offer letter a packet. This gives you the opportunity to get to interns all the information that they will need before they start. Carefully select the material included so that it contains things that interns should know before they arrive rather than everything they will need to know over the course of the internship. Pending availability of the documents, this might include an employee manual, the dress code, the form for intern appraisals so that interns know how they will be evaluated, an internship tip sheet, and any other documents that govern daily operations affecting interns from the outset. There is a careful balance to strike here: While you want interns to have all the information they need to do a good job and to be able to point out that you gave them access to that information, you do not want to overwhelm them with an overabundance of dry, technical documents that they will not take the time to read.

Working with Interns

Working with interns is similar to working with volunteers. As a general rule, prepare for interns, and have their supplies ready for them when they arrive. This maximizes the work they can do in their limited time and makes the organization more productive. After they get started, check with them regularly to make sure their needs are met and that their work is furthering the organization. Finally, thank them regularly so they know they are contributing in a real way to the organization. Beyond these general guidelines, interns require an intensive orientation the first day, thorough training and close supervision, and written evaluations.

Orientation: The Critical First Day

The first day of anything is full of excitement and anxiety, and internships are no exception. This is the start of the period where you will increase the staff and be able to expand the focus of your daily tasks; it is also the start of your commitment to educate a young person. The first day is a critical one for both the organization and interns to get impressions of each other and learn to work together. The information required for a thorough orientation may extend past the first day, so inform the intern that the first few shifts will cover a general orientation to the organization and bridge into task-specific instruction.

To begin, staff members need to decide who will conduct a general orientation to the museum and the way it works. This will likely be the intern's supervisor. Whoever is responsible, it may help to make a checklist to know what to go over with interns when they arrive. While it may seem like you are covering so much information that you may overload the interns, once they learn things one way, it can be difficult to learn it another, "correct" way, so doing it right the first time saves later headaches. When the intern arrives, explain that the first task will be an orientation, and offer pen and paper or other tools to help the student retain the information.

A general orientation should cover the physical facilities, emergency procedures, resources the intern may need to access, and daily expectations. Give interns a clear picture of the lay of the land with a tour of the facility, including both public and restricted areas. Indicate which, if any, areas the intern is not allowed to enter, such as the director's office or collection storage. Also describe how to get into areas that the intern will need to access to complete projects.

For instance, if interns will be working on a collections project, will they access the locked collections storage area with their own keys or will they ask a specific staff member to let them in? This is also the time to show interns basic tasks, such as working the phone systems and accessing computers. Nothing is too basic to point out during orientation; even if interns already know how to do something, the repetition will reinforce the information and remind them that this is important to know.

Emergency preparation is related to a building tour. Because emergencies are so rare, training in this area is an easy thing to overlook. But interns are an integral part of the team and therefore need to know what to do in emergency situations. This is especially true if the intern is working with the public and may be a first responder in a situation involving visitors. Even if the emergency procedure is simply to call a staff member, interns need to know how to reach that person and what information the staff member requires. For instance, if tornado sirens sound with visitors present, what should the intern's first course of action be? Or, more likely, if the interns hear noises in the basement, do they call their intern supervisor? The director? The police? Or do they check it out themselves and report on the situation? Providing a protocol for these types of situations gives interns the tools they need to address situations effectively if an emergency arises. At the very least, interns need to know where first aid materials are located and who should be their first contact in an emergency.

Also show interns the resources they will need to function effectively as part of the organization. Interns fall under the employee or volunteer manual that applies to the rest of the staff in the organization, so make sure that they know which materials they are responsible for knowing. Actually, show them the materials and their location so that interns know what to look for. Providing time during the first few days for interns to look over the materials is one way to ensure that they actually review the information.

This can lead into a discussion of daily expectations. Review what is expected of interns while they are on the job. Timeliness, application to tasks, and revision of work might seem obvious to professional staff, but they are often not so innate to students. Some educational institutions, such as Wabash College, host a mandatory seminar for interns before they begin their internships to set these standards. In the absence of, or in addition to, such a workshop, supervisors need to state these expectations directly. Remember, this often is the first time students have been in a professional setting, and neglecting to spell out the requirements is setting up both the organization and the intern to fail. Cite the form that staff will use to evaluate the intern as a list of expectations.

In a small organization, interns will likely be sharing a workspace with volunteers or paid staff. Work this out ahead of time—there are few things more awkward than an enthusiastic student arriving ready to work and then waiting for you to figure out where he or she is going to sit. Lay out the ground rules for sharing space, such as where interns should put their things when they are not at the museum so that others can work in the space. Does the desk need to be cleared off before the intern leaves? Designate a drawer, bin, or other location where interns can keep their work in progress without leaving it out in someone else's way. Other everyday procedures, such as logging off the computer, are not second nature to a new hire, and interns will do best if you walk them through the procedure the first time. Some organizations, like the General Lew Wallace Study & Museum, have used a time-card system to track intern hours, even when they are not paid a stipend, to allow staff to track project progress and measure intern efficacy and project scope. The orientation period is the time to discuss the time-card form, when and to whom students need to submit it, and how interns will receive payment, if applicable.

The final aspects of orientation deal with the specifics of the project the intern will undertake. If someone else has been orienting the intern, this is the point at which the direct supervisor takes over. Interns need to know where they will be working, what tools they will need to access, and what background information they need to do the job properly. Also acquaint them with the resources, such as reference books, that can help them do their projects. Providing a short time to read about the background of that area of museum work can help give interns a foundation for carrying out the task.

While it may seem that interns spend a great deal of time at the beginning listening and reading rather than doing their projects, this introduction can help expedite the work process when they finally take up their tasks. At the General Lew Wallace Study & Museum, one intern's project entailed entering information from the paper records for the archives and object collections into the computer database. Because there is specific nomenclature for artifacts that a freshman in college would not know, the intern's first task was to sit down with staff-selected readings that discussed nomenclature and object classification. He was then able to recognize the meanings of the fields on the forms and ask more thoughtful questions about the process of entering the information. If you don't provide any background, work that interns do may have to be redone later by someone with more knowledge.

Training and Supervision

Training interns is intensive at the beginning, but after the first few days, it becomes constant yet routine. Interns will likely not have an idea of the larger picture of the organization; it is as though they are stepping into a few frames of the movie of your museum, so they can contribute in a real and meaningful way if you catch them up on what happened before they got there and what you think

99

Photo 4.4. White gloves, artifact marking pens, and condition report forms are all supplies that supervisors need to introduce collections interns to before they start a project.

will happen after they leave. Often, this is as simple as thinking aloud or reviewing a calendar to show when things need to be turned in. When beginning a new task or showing interns something for the first time, asking questions can be a fruitful way of demonstrating a process. Ask what prior knowledge they bring to the table. Even something not directly museum related can be applicable to learning a new task, so build on whatever knowledge you can see the intern has. For instance, a summer job working retail could contribute skills using a cash register, working with customers, and locating items from storage—all skills a museum can use.

Also ask how the intern learns best so that you can maximize instruction time. It is not much good making an active learner sit and listen to an explanation. Often, an effective strategy is for interns to watch a supervisor perform a task first, then have the supervisor talk the intern through it while the intern does it. Give interns clear directions—even have them repeat the process back to you. Introduce them to needed supplies and their locations, especially for items not commonly found outside museums. Ask for questions, and make sure before leaving that both the supervisor and intern are comfortable that the intern can perform all or part of a project. As eager as you might be to get to your own tasks, leaving an intern who has questions will result in undone or poorly done work.

For less hands-on projects, such as researching and writing, supervision may be less intense, but the basics are still the same. Make it clear that you expect drafts and multiple revisions to assure the product is as good as the intern can make it. In turn, the supervisor needs to check in with the intern to assess progress on the project, ask for drafts, set realistic goals and deadlines, and provide

Photo 4.5. Clear directions are essential for interns to succeed.

feedback so interns can improve and learn. Students are used to deadlines, so they may not give a draft to their supervisor unless they know it is expected promptly. It is neither rude nor unexpected to say things like, "This needs to be finished by the end of the week, so please get me a draft by tomorrow so I can make comments and you have time to revise it." For tasks with a longer lead time, ask interns how long they think it will take for them to complete a task; this will not only involve them in setting a realistic deadline but increase their time management skills.

Checking in also gives more timid interns an opportunity to ask questions. Some might be too shy to interrupt your work and would prefer that supervisors approach them or oversee their work closely. Margaret Ott learned this first-hand: "We had one intern working with the collection, and I thought I could train her and then she could work by herself. But she wasn't comfortable being in our old jail building by herself, and the other volunteers didn't feel comfortable supervising work they don't usually do, so I ended up working a lot more hours. Even though that was the biggest challenge for our all-volunteer organization, I thought it was worth it, so I put in the time." Occasionally, some interns may be surfing the Internet or doing unrelated schoolwork on museum computers, taking time and resources away from the project at hand. Walking by and talking to the intern will limit these occurrences, though in some cases interns will need to be reminded—politely but firmly—of policies or expectations.

Feedback is a regular aspect of intern supervision. In addition to appraisals at the midpoint and end of the internship, interns need feedback so that they can adjust their behavior and performance according to expectations. Comments on drafts, verbal correction as necessary, and periodic checking with interns about how they see the progress of their projects all makes the entire internship a learning experience. Saving feedback, either positive or negative, for appraisal time only increases apprehension about the review and takes the comments out of the context in which correction is needed, lessening the learning opportunity. Feedback should be clear, concise, and compassionate. Long and flowery phrases or jokes to dull the sting of a reproach can send mixed signals and make the feedback less effective. Stating your observation, giving the reason for the correction, and asking the intern to fix the problem will communicate the message. For instance, you can say, "Steve, I noticed your lunch dishes were still in the sink. We all need to wash our own dishes so bugs don't get into the museum, so please go take care of that." Keep in mind that interns are students rather than consummate professionals, and some compassion and sense of a learning curve are needed.

Student status is no excuse, however, for repeated offenses, and there may be times when disciplinary measures are needed. Interns need to follow the established code of conduct, and the steps that you would normally take to discipline a wayward staff member are the same as those used to discipline an intern. As part of the learning experience, the correction for the mistake may require great effort on the intern's part. For example, breaches of the dress code will likely not recur if the intern is sent home to change. Document reprimands or repeated offenses and keep a record in the intern's file. This will provide a paper trail for midpoint and terminal evaluations, as well as for any final report the college needs. It is rare but possible to dismiss an intern who is truly ineffective, hostile, or otherwise just not working out. Most organizations decide that whatever work the intern does outweighs the problems caused by the firing process and subsequent lack of labor. Check with the college or university about other re-courses, as well as the payment of credits or stipends, before firing interns.

Evaluating the Experience

Feedback is a daily occurrence during internships, but interns should also be appraised in writing, ideally once at the approximate midpoint and again at the end of the internship. Some colleges require specific evaluation forms. Internships through IUPUI, the University of Indianapolis, and Ball State University's Public History Program have a three-part evaluation: students rate their experiences, museum staff rate the students' performance, and the faculty advisors rate the overall experience. Even when a specific form is not required, Morris-Butler House Museum supervisors still evaluate interns in writing with a formal letter. Similarly, Noble County Historical Society volunteers who supervise interns appraise intern performance based on requirements for the grants that funded the internships. The General Lew Wallace Study & Museum evaluates interns in the middle of internships and again at the end. The midpoint appraisal gives both the intern and the supervisor a chance to assess performance and provide direction for the remainder of the internship. There should be notable progress between the two appraisals.

A standard form can help make the appraisal process quick and standard. Use both open-ended questions and ratings of performance characteristics. This allows supervisors to express their impression of working with the intern in their own words while still giving information in a standardized way. For the ratings portion, break down the various characteristics the organization as an employer looks for in its workers. These include specific behaviors a supervisor wants to see in an employee who will work on a project, relate to coworkers, and interact with the public. Rate these on a scale of one to four, and include "N/A" for categories that do not apply (for instance, an intern who does not work with the public cannot be evaluated on customer service skills).

SAMPLE EVALUATION QUESTIONS FOR INTERNS

Open-Ended Questions
- Has the intern's performance met initial expectations? Explain.
- Why was the intern initially hired to work at the museum?
- What are some notable characteristics of the intern's performance?
- In what ways can the intern improve his or her performance?

Characteristics to Rate
- *Work ethic:* time management, professional dress, attitude, attention to detail, quality of finished products
- *Employee relations:* visitor services, working as part of a team, following directions, utilizing constructive criticism
- *Museum concerns:* stewardship of historic artifacts, researching historical information, making the museum relevant or blending the past and present

Everyone who supervises the intern—not everyone who works with the intern—fills out the form, and then the intern coordinator condenses the information in a summary of the staff opinion. Intern supervisors may or may not be the same people every time. For example, an intern in collections would be appraised by the collections manager, while an intern in educational programs would be appraised by the staff in charge of education. Be careful of asking volunteers to evaluate interns; this is a staff job, so only involve volunteers if they staff the organization. After all the appropriate staffers have evaluated the intern, they return their forms to the staff person in charge of coordinating internships, who then combines the feedback into a summary of the staff's opinion. This presents a united front on the part of the organization and prevents hard feelings targeted toward one individual who gave a bad review. A paper copy of the summary appraisal should be signed by the intern coordinator, the intern's supervisor, the museum director, and the intern. The signatures attest that everyone has been apprised of the progress of the internship and direction for improvement. A less formal alternative is for the staff person who coordinates internships to talk with the intern's direct supervisor about the intern's performance and to incorporate those impressions in a written document.

To deliver the news, set up a time to meet face-to-face so the intern recognizes that this is important. Print out two final copies of the summary appraisal for the review: one for the intern and one for you to talk from. Sit down with the intern in a quiet place to minimize distractions and encourage dialogue. As much as this is a time for the organization to point out areas for improvement, it is also a time for the intern to ask questions and clarify misunderstandings. Describe the process used to complete the appraisal, and make it clear that this evaluation does not come solely from one person. Hand the intern a copy of the appraisal. This is especially important for more visual learners. Going over a printed document can also make the appraisal seem more official. It is tough to sit people down and tell them what they are doing incorrectly, but this is supposed to be a learning experience for interns. They should expect to receive some correction, and even if they do not expect it, it does not help either the intern or the organization if you only tell them good things without providing any feedback on ways to improve.

As you review the appraisal, make sure to balance comments so that they include aspects of performance that the staff is pleased with as well as areas that need improvement. Use concrete examples when possible. An appraisal might go something like this: "Overall, we're really happy with your work performance. You're really good at research, and you ask questions when you don't understand how to do something. One area for improvement is contributing to the work environment, like making sure your lunch dishes are cleaned and your workspace is clear when you leave for the day. Overall, you're doing a good job, and we think your project will be a great asset when it's finished."

Finally, encourage questions from the intern. Often interns do not have questions at an appraisal meeting because they have never before been evaluated in this way. Even if no questions are forthcoming, encourage the intern to take a minute to think, and then keep the offer on the table to come back—in person or even via e-mail—if questions do come to mind. Repeat this appraisal process at the end of the internship, and point out specific areas that have improved from the last appraisal.

In addition to reviewing interns' performance, ask them for feedback on their internship experiences. Filling out a form with both open-ended and rating questions gives them a chance to reflect on their internship and gives the organization an idea of what students are getting from the experience. Let the students use the form to evaluate things as they see them before sitting down for a midpoint or final appraisal meeting. After the meeting, review the intern's evaluation form. This order of operations prevents the organization's review from coloring the students' perspective or vice versa.

TEXTBOX 4.7

FEEDBACK FROM INTERNS

Open-Ended Questions
- Why did you decide to intern at the museum?
- Has the internship experience met your initial expectations? Explain.
- Please describe your experience (provide space for positive and negative comments).
- In what ways could your internship improve?

How Has Your Internship Helped You?
- Provide a checklist of skills interns often develop, such as met new people, gained job experience, and increased knowledge of local history.
- Ask intern to rate characteristics such as work ethic, time management, professional dress, attitude, attention to detail, and quality of finished products.

Record Keeping

Maintaining a file for each intern will keep all the paperwork associated with each person in one place. The intern and the sponsoring institution also need copies of documents pertaining to the internship. For the museum's file, retain a copy of the offer letter to function as a written contract. That way, if an intern wants to change the scope of a project or work a different number of hours than the organization needs, you have something in writing to refer back to the original agreement between the intern and organization. Also keep a copy of the job description, any notes taken during the interview process, and a copy of the intern appraisal signed by the intern, the supervisor, and the organization director. Finally, intern files are places to keep documentation of anything that led up to comments on appraisals, both reprimands and samples of excellent work. For instance, if an intern had a problem with timeliness and e-mailed to explain absences, copies of those e-mails would provide a paper trail for that issue. Similarly, if a visitor wrote a thank-you note to praise a tour received from the intern, then that is more documentation of the intern's performance. If the museum funds interns through a grant, keep copies of paperwork for the final grant report.

Students often do not know what to do with paperwork, so keep to a minimum what you give to interns for their personal records. They should receive a copy of the initial offer letter and each appraisal to retain for themselves. To the sponsoring college or university, give a copy of signed intern appraisals and anything else required for the institution's internship program, such as time cards, samples of the intern's work, or a final report. The sponsoring institution does not need documentation of anything that led up to comments on the appraisal unless it requests this. By meeting the obligations to the sponsoring institution, you are likely to build a long-lasting relationship between the museum and the college.

Success

Looking at all that is involved, creating an internship program certainly seems like a lot of work. It is worthwhile, however, as a way to increase organizational productivity and give students needed experience. The organization can begin to think strategically by planning intern projects, completing work, and meeting goals with the extra labor and skill that interns provide. Interns, in turn, receive valuable experience, course credit or a stipend, and a solid education in museum work.

Interns have helped small places do large projects. "One intern through Ball State University worked extensively with the photograph collection of a small historical society, and his work helped both the local and a state organization. The student organized the photographs by topic, stored them in acid-free folders, researched and wrote a descriptive caption for each, cataloged them in an electronic database program, and digitized them for posting on the museum's website," according to supervising faculty member Dr. Michael William Doyle.

Another success story comes from the Morris-Butler House Museum. Staffed by one part-time and two full-time employees, Morris-Butler relies heavily on volunteers and has hosted interns for several years. Former intern Amanda McGuire recalled that her supervisor informed her during the interview that the museum was small and that everyone had to complete many different types of tasks. Her main responsibility was to give scheduled and walk-in tours for the public and, between tours, to assist with other daily operations. "I did a little bit of everything, from preparing materials for board meetings to cutting out newspaper articles about the museum," she said. Other interns have assisted with behind-the-scenes goals, including inventorying the entire collection. This project, which included noting locations and reporting conditions, was planned for an academic year so the intern had enough time to complete it. Morris-Butler hosts as many as three interns simultaneously throughout the year, with projects in public programming, education, research, and exhibit fabrication. "The real success," concluded project coordinator Aimee Rose Formo, "is that several of our interns have come back to volunteer. They want to come back and continue helping."

The Noble County Historical Society's Margaret Ott agreed that interns are worth the investment: "I never would have gotten caught up on many things had I not had interns. I couldn't have done that much by myself, and we don't have enough volunteers. I was willing to put in the time to train interns and supervise them because they helped us get so much done." As an all-volunteer museum, the organization faced particular challenges in finding supervisors and grants to pay interns an hourly wage. Not only did they overcome these challenges with planning, but they also learned from inevitable missteps. "At first we didn't time things as well as we could have," Ott said. "But the second year we knew the process and used our intern more effectively. We've had a lot of success as time goes on."

The excellent track records and positive experiences of the Morris-Butler House Museum, Noble County Historical Society, and many other small museums demonstrate that even with a small or all-volunteer staff, the patient and diligent process of starting an internship program will lay the foundation and pave the way for future interns and organizational success.

MANY HANDS MAKE LIGHT WORK: STRENGTH THROUGH COLLABORATION

Eileen McHugh

Why Collaborate?

- Times are hard; we need all the help we can get.
- Sharing resources helps them go further.
- Collaboration can increase your audience.
- Collaboration can make your project more attractive to grant-making agencies.

Maintaining the financial health of a small nonprofit organization has never been easy. Smaller organizations are used to making the most of what resources are available, getting by with less, and striving to have the biggest impact with the smallest cost. But even with very careful fiscal management, it seems to be getting harder every day to make ends meet. The financial crisis that began in 2009 will shape the future of museums for years, perhaps decades, to come. The recession has negatively affected every traditional source of museum funding. With local municipalities, the states, and the federal government facing huge deficits, securing museum funding from the government has become more challenging than ever. Even well-funded museums with long-established relationships with their local governments are no longer able to rely on governmental funding. Many small museums are actually at risk of closing their doors forever.

Foundation funding, long a major source of museum revenue, has also been affected. The general steep decline of the stock market has decreased the value of most foundation endowments. Since foundations routinely distribute grants based on a percentage of their endowment's total value, foundation grants have decreased across the board. More organizations are seeking funding at a time when there is less funding to distribute. The competition is getting stiffer for a smaller slice of the pie.

Private funding, or donations from individual donors, is also becoming more difficult to secure. Until the economy is clearly recovering from what is now being called the Great Recession, many people are decreasing their expenditures across the board. Even many long-time museum supporters are cutting back on donations at a time when our institutions need them more than ever. How can we survive?

Collaboration with other organizations can be the answer, or at least part of the answer. By partnering with other like-minded organizations, our museums can share resources. When paying for services, like the cost of a professional consultant or the rental of specialized equipment, the cost is decreased when spread across a number of participating partners. This can make the difference between being able to afford something and having to do without it. By allowing another organization access to your museum's resources—gallery space, the professional expertise of your director, even your volunteer force—you may gain access to that other organization's resources. Presumably, most of these resources will be available at little or no cost, becoming a way to increase your museum's capital without adding to the operating budget.

The funding organizations on which museums rely—from federal and state agencies, private foundations, and even individual donors—has given way to collaboration as a way of making dollars stretch further. Many of these funding organizations actively encourage partnerships among grant seekers, awarding extra points in the evaluation process for collaborative projects. Collaboration can literally mean the difference between staying afloat and going under in difficult times.

Collaboration can give you access to new ideas and new energy. You will have more people thinking about how to solve a problem or achieve a particular goal, more people bringing their talents, skills, and experience to the service of your museum. Dividing a task into pieces and spreading them over a wider group of willing participants has to lighten the load for everyone.

Collaboration can be valuable to your museum in other ways. When you partner with another organization, you spread the word about your museum to the members of that organization. When you begin the process of collaboration with another organization, you begin enlarging your museum community. People who have never been through your doors will learn about what you are doing and why it matters. Your work will be exposed to new audiences, whom you will have the opportunity to convert into genuine supporters. Ideally, you will be strengthening the other organization as well, which can strengthen your entire community. Collaboration is good for all of us.

How to Begin

The first steps toward a successful collaboration are examination and conversation. You must be fully aware of your own museum's strengths and weaknesses before you can choose an organization with which to partner. Your museum must have a clear mission statement. You must know who you are and what you are doing. If your museum has not yet taken the time to think about and formulate its mission statement, you are not yet ready to collaborate with anyone else. Self-examination, through meetings with your board, interested members of your community (now called stakeholders), and past trustees will give you a clearer picture of where your museum stands today and where you want it to be in the future. Your mission statement should express this.

To be done well, this cannot be a quick process. You must examine your museum closely. What has worked for you in the past? What has not? If you are a collecting institution, what is unique about your holdings? What do you have to offer another organization? You should consider your membership. Who in your community believes in and supports your museum? Why? What do these people see as the museum's purpose? How engaged is your museum with the community, and what is your profile within it? Are people aware of you and what you are doing?

Does your museum have a paid staff? If so, is the staff aware of best practices in museums? If not, is the governing body of your museum aware of and engaged in museum best practices? What museum resources are available to you in your state?

If you have not yet begun the process of self-examination, the American Association of Museums offers the Museum Assessment Program to guide you through with the help of a professional peer. The American Association for State and Local History offers the Standards and Excellence Program for History Organizations (StEPS), a self-paced, self-study assessment program for small and midsize organizations. More information on both of these programs is available in chapter 1 of Book 1 of this series and from the organizations' websites.

What Kinds of Collaborations?

There are as many kinds of successful collaborations as there are museums: programming partnerships, fundraising events, Web-based projects, marketing initiatives, and many more. You may partner with another organization to raise funds for a specific purpose. A history museum and the history club at the high school may write and perform a play to raise money for the restoration of a particular object. Your museum may collaborate with one or more other museums on a new exhibition. Several museums in your area might collaborate on creating an exhibition about one particular ethnic group, with the exhibition to travel from one museum to the next throughout the region. Your museum could collaborate with a museum at a great distance from you that holds collections similar to yours. Your house museum might collaborate with several other museums throughout the country to put a digital catalog of your decorative arts collection online. You could partner with a local organization to increase both your audiences. A local barbershop quartet may provide the musical entertainment at the opening reception for your new museum exhibit. The list of ideas for potential partnerships is nearly endless.

Identify Potential Partners

The most successful collaborations are among organizations with similar missions. Many communities or regions have more than one museum with a similar mission. Local history museums, for example, are designed to preserve and interpret the history of that area. A historic house museum and a historic society at not too great a distance from each other will almost surely have similar missions. Art museums and art supply stores may have similar missions of celebrating the creative arts in their communities. A natural history museum and local outdoors clubs may have similar missions of preserving and appreciating the flora and fauna of their area. All types of museums have formed successful partnerships with local school districts. The core mission of every school district is education, just as education is frequently a part of a museum's mission. When missions align, it is fairly easy to create collaborations that can further the missions of all partners.

Successful partnerships can also be formed between organizations with complementary missions—goals that support one another but are not necessarily the same. Most senior centers, for example, seek to keep senior citizens actively engaged in the life of their communities. Many types of museums can help the senior centers achieve that goal while furthering the museum's mission as well. For example, collecting oral histories at senior centers can serve to validate the senior residents as contributing members of the community while providing the museum with primary source material it would be impossible to obtain anywhere else.

Many museums have a key goal of bringing people into their establishments, an aim that is complementary to those of tourism agencies and tourism-related businesses: restaurants, retail stores, hotels, motels and B&Bs, and transportation companies. The more people are attracted to an area because of a museum's profile, the likelier they are to avail themselves of the services of the local businesses that rely on tourists.

Fertile ground for successful collaborations can be found in the unmet needs in your community. Museums may be able to partner with human service organizations to help meet the challenges of a particular demographic group in your area. After-school programs, at either the museum or another site, serve the needs of the community in many ways: creating a safe, fun, and educational place for children to be after school, solving at least part of the child-care dilemma of many working parents, and engaging a new audience for museum programming. Perhaps a geographic district within your community is underutilized. Many museums, even those on the outskirts of town, have collaborated successfully with downtown business organizations. Museums present off-site programs downtown, bringing people back to the neighborhoods that are still perceived as the hearts of our communities. Sometimes museum collaboration can help meet the needs of an individual. Is there a performer, a lecturer, an artist, or an author in your community whose work aligns with the thematic areas of the museum? By working with the museum, the presenter can build a new audience for his or her work, while exposing more people to the museum and its mission.

Look to your museum's historic associations for ideas for potential partners for future collaborations. Which people and organizations helped start the museum? Who were your earliest supporters? Social and fraternal organizations are often longtime supporters of local museums; yet many museum directors do not think of moving from a supplicant relationship to an actual partnership on a project or program. Perhaps you can collaborate successfully with organizations within your community that relate to a particular aspect of your collection or programming. A local watercolor society, for example, may be interested in raising funds for the conservation of watercolor paintings in your collection. A local reenactors' group may be interested in providing living history programs at your museum around the anniversary of specific events.

Creating Successful Partnership Programs

It is not easy to examine your own museum in light of its strengths and weaknesses, past successes and failures, and community and individual relationships. Nor is it easy to know your community so well that you know which organizations have missions similar or complementary to yours. We are really talking about how well you know your community, the people, the players, the resources, and the challenges. The better your organization knows its community, the more adeptly it will build successful partnerships within that community.

Which comes first, identifying a potential partner or outlining the collaborative project? The short answer is either. Sometimes you will know that you want your museum to work with a specific organization, based on the reasons outlined above, and you will create a project that will benefit you both. Other times, you will have a project in mind that you want to complete for your museum, and you will go looking for others to help make it happen. Whichever way the project starts, some of the same things must happen to make it successful.

The goals of the project must meet the needs of all partners. To put it bluntly, all must get something out of it. It is not crass or commercial to think, when approached about a partnership opportunity, "What's in it for me?" The collaboration must be designed in such a way that each partner benefits. Each partner must be clear about what it wants to realize from the project. By taking the time to discuss the goals of a particular project, you will be defining what each of the participants wants to get out of it. This will help in planning to reach those goals.

Be specific and realistic. If possible, quantify your goals. One shared goal of a public event may be to attract public attention to your respective organizations. What does that mean? Do you want to attract five hundred people to the event? One thousand? Do you want the event covered by the local media? By clearly defining the goals, you lay the groundwork for the next step: determining who will do what and how.

The project, whether simple or complex, short-lived or long-term, must have clear, achievable goals. These goals should, wherever possible, be based on the actual experience of the partnering organizations. The conversation about any possible collaboration must begin with a discussion of what each partner brings to the project and expects to get out of it. What each organization takes away may be very different—one may get a new audience, one may reap financial benefits, and one may gain access to new equipment—but all partners need to be clear about what they expect. A successful collaboration must be a win-win for all involved.

When outlined, the project should include a division of resources and rewards. No one wants to do more than his share of the work, and no one wants anyone else to get all the benefits. Clear planning, with specifics about who does what, who pays for what, and how everything is to be divided, is essential. (See textbox 5.1 for a sample partnership agreement.) Whether the partners are paying for the project themselves or they are seeking outside funding, identifying all the necessary funding sources should be part of the initial planning. The project plan should outline the project, define the goals, list all the major tasks and who will perform them by what date, and who will pay for what. These project outlines, with specific goals, task assignments, and time lines, should be in writing, distributed to all partners, and updated regularly from conception through execution to evaluation.

EXAMPLE PARTNERSHIP AGREEMENT: FINGER LAKES VACATIONS PROJECT

The _____ agrees to participate as a partner in the Finger Lakes Vacation Project being submitted to the Institute of Library and Museum Services (IMLS). As a partner, we agree to

1. commit staff and volunteer time as shown in the project budget;
2. provide documentation of that time and other expenses to the project director for reporting purposes;
3. take the lead or assist in submitting additional applications for project support;
4. work as a team in creating the core exhibitions, public and school programs, and marketing efforts;
5. use our own initiative, staff time, and skills in creating the site-based exhibition at our facility, while sharing information, collections (objects and archival materials), and skills with all project partners;
6. participate in an effective evaluation process, the exact nature of which will be determined upon the successful receipt of grant funds; and
7. participate as a willing partner in working with the Yates County Genealogical and Historical Society and all project partners to meet the goals of the project and of the IMLS Learning Opportunity grants.

The Yates County Genealogical and Historical Society agrees to

1. serve as the lead agency for the project and take responsibility for project management, financial management, and grant reporting;
2. coordinate the work of the partnership; and
3. provide all partners with relevant financial and other grant information.

_____   _____
CEO of each partner organization   Date

_____   _____
Director, Yates County Genealogical and Historical Society   Date

As mentioned earlier, collaborative projects are often more attractive to potential funders than individual projects. As tempting as it is, you should resist finding a partner and creating a project simply because the funding seems to be available. This is another reason why a clearly defined mission statement is so important. Your museum needs to work on achieving its mission, not undertaking whichever project seems most likely to be funded. Often referred to as "chasing the money," creating a project simply because you know you can get it funded is not going to move your museum forward. That is why the project planning, a detailed outline of goals, and the examination of whether the project meets the needs of all partners must come before the development of funds for the project. You may have difficulty explaining this concept to board members or others in your community who see any funding as desirable, but you simply have to convey the importance of keeping your programming mission driven. One collaborative project that does not further the museum's mission may not derail the museum's momentum. But a succession of projects that are not closely aligned with the mission and the strategic plan may put your museum in danger of "losing itself"—becoming an organization with no clear purpose in your community.

What to Watch Out For

Just as the adage "Many hands make light work" can be applied to successful collaborations, the saying "Too many cooks spoil the soup" can apply to failed collaborations. A collaboration, by its very nature, entails a group of people working together to achieve common goals. If group members have contradictory goals or cannot work together, the collaboration is doomed.

The importance of defining achievable goals, agreed upon by all partners, has been discussed. Equally important is agreeing on who will do what and when. Requirements for all partners should be established at the beginning of the planning process. Partners should be aware of the consequences if the requirements are not met. Regular updates to the project's status, distributed to all partners, can alleviate any unpleasant surprises. Partner organizations should make sure that their internal systems, boards, and other staff members are aware and supportive of the collaborative project.

Did It Work?

All project partners should be involved in creating a written evaluation of the collaborative project and its outcomes. The first step in evaluating the success of any collaboration is to examine whether each partner's goals were met.

Your attention to setting specific goals in the planning stage of the project is important here. If you know exactly what you expect to get out of a collaboration, you will not be left wondering whether it succeeded or not. Each partner can do a part of this evaluation, or a designated person from one of the participating organizations can do the entire report. The report should review any unexpected challenges or benefits that arose during the course of the collaboration. Did unforeseen problems arise with equipment, partners, or funders? Did everything run smoothly? Even if no outside funding is involved, a written evaluation (along the lines of a final report to a funding agency) will be helpful to the partners in future planning.

The evaluation should consider whether the collaboration can be ongoing. If it was, indeed, successful, can it be continued? Collaboration between two or more museums on a specific exhibition may end with that particular exhibit. But if the partnership worked well for that exhibit theme, it may work just as well for another one. If your museum and another organization with a similar mission created a series of programs that attracted large audiences this year, can you create a second series of programs for next year?

The evaluation should also consider whether the collaboration can be duplicated. Collaboration between a group of museums from different parts of the country to put a decorative arts catalog online could be duplicated for their costume or painting collections. A partnership among two or more cultural organizations working together in one community may work just as well among the cultural organizations in another community. If a collaboration has, in fact, worked very well, the person who writes the final evaluation may consider sharing the information about that successful project publicly through the museum press or a museum blog. In the words of C. C. Colton, "Imitation is the sincerest form of flattery."

Collaboration Case Studies

City of Auburn's Historic and Cultural Sites Commission

The city of Auburn, New York, has four independently operated historic sites within 1.5 miles of each other within the city limits: the Cayuga Museum of History and Art, the Harriet Tubman Home, the Seward House, and the Willard Memorial Chapel. Auburn, a city of about twenty-eight thousand people in upstate New York, faces many of the same issues as other Rust Belt cities: declining population, lack of jobs, empty factory buildings, and a declining downtown. In 1998, the directors of the four historic sites met to begin discussing ways in which they could collaborate to promote their institutions. Calling themselves the Historic Sites Task Force, the directors focused on convincing the city council to form—and fund—a commission to help promote the sites. The mission of the task force was "to present a case document to the Auburn City Council in April 1999 providing background information and development guidelines for the creation of a Historic Park Commission for the city of Auburn, N.Y." The site directors met several times to brainstorm how they could convince the city councilors of the value of their plan, gather the statistics on how the historic sites were already attracting people to the city, and show how promoting the historic sites would benefit the entire community.

In January 2000, the city of Auburn transformed the temporary task force into a permanent Historic Sites Commission (HSC) and funded it with $50,000 from the city budget. The mission of HSC was "to develop and implement an integrated tourism strategy for the City of Auburn, N.Y. by creating an action plan to market, promote and host special events linking all of the City's historic sites." With the inception of the HSC, the group began to meet monthly on a regular schedule and formed working committees to address specific goals: planning and development, marketing, events and nominating. In the same month that the HSC was officially created, the Planning and Development Committee applied to the New York State Arts and Business Council for a Cultural Tourism Grant for the HSC's first project.

The project, called Dreams, Discovery, and Design, was a partnership among the city of Auburn, the Cayuga County Tourism Office, and the four historic sites. The city contributed $25,000 from its annual budget. The tourism office contributed $4,550. The grant from the Arts and Business Council was $23,800, for a total of $53,350. The entire project was designed to bring both local and tourist attention to the four participating museums. The HSC created a website promoting the city's historic sites (TourAuburnNY.com), placed ads in national magazines, created a brochure that would be mailed to respondents to the ads, and produced a bumper sticker promoting the website to be given out locally. The project included hiring the members of Auburn High School's Living History Players—costumed interpreters—to portray famous Auburn residents at the historic sites. The project created an Ambassador Program to inform local tourism service providers about the historic sites and encourage them to relay this information to visitors. The stated goal of the project was to increase out-of-town visitors to the historic sites, as measured by overnight occupancy in area lodgings.

One of the major benefits of the partnership was the pooling of resources. The marketing and promotional expertise of the tourism staff became available to the members of the HSC on a regular basis. No one site could afford to advertise in national magazines like *Yankee* or *Better Homes and Gardens*. Similarly, no one site could afford to develop and pay for the Living History Players program. By becoming a part of the partnership, each historic site gained national

Figure 5.1. This ad for the member sites of Auburn's Historical and Cultural Sites Commission ran in *Better Homes and Gardens*, and other national publications. None of the sites could have afforded this type of advertising on their own.

exposure, widespread distribution of promotional materials, a well-organized and artistic program on-site through the summer months, and the expertise of tourism professionals.

The committee structure of the HSC allowed the various site directors to serve in the capacity that best utilized their skills and experience, at the same time giving the other site directors access to those skills and experiences. For example, the director of the Willard Memorial Chapel, who had done the most business with bus-tour operators, shared her experience and contacts with other commission members. The director of the Seward House, who had used the Living History Players the most often, helped design interpretive programs for each site.

The HSC's Dreams, Discovery, and Design project was an unqualified success. During its initial twelve-month period, revenue from the hotel bed tax in the project area went up 19 percent! Both local and out-of-town visitation increased sharply at each of the historic sites. The press coverage of the project and its results was uniformly positive. The project made local residents aware of the economic importance of marketing the area's cultural heritage.

Since its formation, Auburn's HSC has continued to market Auburn's cultural sites successfully. Its name was changed to the Historic and Cultural Sites Commission in 2007 to reflect the admission of two nonhistoric institutions to the partnership, the Schweinfurth Memorial Art Center and the Auburn Public

Theater. The city of Auburn continues to fund the commission (in 2010 giving $50,000) to create a unified marketing campaign to promote all the city's cultural attractions. The website is professionally maintained and updated regularly, and the brochure has gone through numerous print runs of fifty thousand each. The members of the HSC continue to meet each month to collaborate on joint promotions, special events, and sharing expertise.

The Summer in the Finger Lakes Exhibit

The fourteen-county Finger Lakes region is a beautiful, mainly rural area of upstate New York, where residents and tourists have been vacationing for more than 150 years. In early 2001, a group of curators, educators, and directors from six Finger Lakes history museums met to begin exploring the development of a collaborative project that would examine both historic and contemporary tourism in the region. The participating museums are the History Center (Ithaca), the Cayuga Museum of History and Art (Auburn), the Geneva Historical Society (Geneva), the Ontario County Historical Society (Canandaigua), the Glenn H. Curtiss Museum (Hammondsport), and the Yates County Genealogical and Historical Society (Penn Yan).

During the meeting, the initial conversation resulted in both exhibition and program ideas, as well as a list of minimum requirements for involvement on the part of the six participating museums. In a series of meetings, the group decided to share responsibilities for developing project funding. The Geneva Historical Society wrote two successful grant proposals for the project: a National Endowment for the Humanities (NEH) Consultant Grant and an exhibition planning grant from the New York State Council on the Arts (NYSCA). The NYSCA grant allowed for the hiring of museum consultant Linda Norris of Riverhill, who had extensive experience with small museums in upstate New York, and a professional exhibit designer. The NEH grant allowed for the hiring of scholars to meet with the museum group to develop the exhibit's interpretive themes. Norris conducted preliminary research, held oral history training workshops, conducted oral history interviews, and developed outlines for the core and individual exhibits. A brochure seeking input from the public on the exhibit's themes was distributed at each of the six participating museums. Through several meetings, the plan was developed to create an exhibit in six parts. Each segment would feature twelve exhibit panels exploring a different aspect of vacationing in the Finger Lakes. Each participating museum would host one segment of the exhibit each summer for six years. In 2003, the group submitted an application to the Institute of Museum and Library Services (IMLS) to fund the production of the actual exhibit. The application was turned down.

Another meeting of staff from the participating museums was held. The IMLS reviewers' remarks were distributed and discussed. Since two of the reviewers were very positive, the decision was made to revamp the project plans slightly and submit the application again. In 2006, the project was resubmitted to the IMLS Museums for America grant program, as well as to the New York Council for the Humanities (NYCH). Both applications were successful.

The total budget for the project was $81,725. The IMLS grant was $53,425, and the NYCH grant was $7,800. This left each of the six participating museums with a cost share of $3,416, quite a bargain for a professionally designed, locally focused exhibit each year for six years. Once the funding was secured, consultant Linda Norris gathered the historic photographs from each participating museum, commissioned contemporary photographs, designed the exhibit, and wrote the exhibit text, minimizing the workload for the staff at each museum, while producing an extremely well-designed exhibit. One very successful part of the design has been Norris's idea to use screen doors as the display stands. The nostalgic-looking screen doors are joined together in sets of three. The exhibit panels fit into the top part of the doors (where the screens would go). When the time comes to rotate the panels from one museum to another, only the panels, which fit easily into a car, have to be moved. The doors themselves fold together to be stored flat when not in use.

An interesting aspect of this project is that the staffs at many of the six participating museums changed during the five years between the start of the conversation and the awarding of the IMLS grant. Clear agreements during the initial meetings as to which museum was responsible for what aided in the continuation of the project as it passed through different staff hands. Board-approved letters of commitment to the project also showed the funding agencies that each museum was committed, even if the staff had changed. As of this writing the exhibit is more than halfway through the six-year rotation of its segments, and it has proved very popular with visitors throughout the region.

Getting Stronger Together

Collaborative projects can help build your museum into a more connected, better funded, more vital institution. Working together with other individuals and organizations can make your museum even more of an asset to your community. Other like-minded people nearby value the work you are doing, or your museum would not be where it is today. Find those people. Begin the conversation about what you are trying to achieve and what others are working toward. There are probably ways you can work together. By pooling your resources, sharing ideas, and dividing a big job into many smaller tasks, you can generate new enthusiasm, build your audience, and benefit your museum and your organization in any number of ways. In short, collaboration lets you do more with less. Successful collaborations can create a better museum.

APPENDIX A

Oberlin Heritage Center

P.O. Box 0455

73 ½ S. Professor Street

Oberlin, OH 44074

APPLICATION FOR EMPLOYMENT

AN EQUAL OPPORTUNITY EMPLOYER

PLEASE READ BEFORE COMPLETING THIS APPLICATION. IN READ-ING AND ANSWERING THE FOLLOWING QUESTIONS, PLEASE KEEP IN MIND THAT NONE OF THE QUESTIONS IS INTENDED TO IMPLY ANY LIMITATIONS, PREFERENCES, OR DISCRIMINATION BASED ON ANY NON-JOB-RELATED INFORMATION. COMPLETION OF THIS APPLICATION DOES NOT ENSURE EMPLOYMENT; HOWEVER, IF A SUITABLE OPENING OCCURS, THIS APPLICATION MAY RECEIVE DUE CONSIDERATION. USE OF THIS FORM DOES NOT INDICATE THERE ARE POSITIONS AVAILABLE.

APPENDIX A

PLEASE PRINT

I. PERSONAL DATA

Name: _____

        Last   First   Middle

Address: _____

       Street   City   State   Zip

Phone at which you can be reached: (___)_____ (___)_____

                                    Daytime   Evening

Previous address (if you resided less than two years at the above):

_____

Street   City   State   Zip

If hired, can you provide proof of right to work in the United States?

                                               ___ Yes ___ No

Position(s) applied for: _____

___ Full-time   ___ Part-time   ___ Temporary

Hours preferred _____

Date available for work: _____

Are you at least eighteen?   ___ Yes ___ No

If not, can you submit a work permit?   ___ Yes ___ No

II. EDUCATION AND TRAINING

School	Name and Address	Major Courses	Graduated or Degree
High school			
College			
Graduate school			
Trade or business			
Other			

Describe any other experience, training, skills, academic or professional honors, publications, grants, professional memberships, and licenses or certificates. Attach additional sheets if necessary. _____

_____

_____

_____

_____

III. WORK HISTORY

List all previous employment. Start with the most recent. Attach additional sheets if necessary.

Employer Name, Address, and Phone Number	Supervisor's Name	Final Position	Ending Salary	Reason for Leaving	Dates of Employment

IV. MILITARY SERVICE

Have you served in the U.S. Armed Forces?   ___ Yes   ___ No

Branch of service: _____   Length of service: _____

Indicate service school attended or other special training received: _____

_____

V. MISCELLANEOUS

Would you be willing to travel (statewide or otherwise) should your position require you to?   ___ Yes   ___ No

In what career field within Oberlin Heritage Center do you desire to work?

_____

Have you ever applied to work here before?   ___ Yes ___ No

Position applied for: _____ When? _____

Have you ever worked here before?   ___ Yes ___ No
If yes, please explain: _____

Have you ever been convicted of a crime that may relate to the position for which you are applying?   ___ Yes ___ No
If so, explain: _____

_____

NOTE: The existence of a criminal record does not create an automatic bar to employment.

VI. REFERENCES

Please provide three references who are not relatives.

Name, Address, and Phone Number	Known How Long	Occupation

PLEASE READ CAREFULLY

EXAMINE YOUR APPLICATION BEFORE SIGNING TO SEE THAT YOU HAVE GIVEN AN ANSWER TO EACH ITEM.

I certify that the facts set forth in this employment application (and any accompanying resume) are true and complete to the best of my knowledge. I understand that any falsification, omission, misrepresentation, or concealment of information on this application may be sufficient grounds for disqualification from further consideration for hire or immediate discharge and that the organization shall not be liable in any respect if my employment is so denied or terminated.

I authorize the organization to verify the information contained in this application and to investigate my personal or employment history. I also authorize any former school, employer, person, firm, corporation, or government agency to give the organization information it may have about me. In consideration of the organization's review of this application, I release the organization and all providers of information from any liability as a result of furnishing and receiving this information.

I further agree that if employed, I will conform my conduct to the organization's employment rules. I understand that no personnel recruiter, interviewer, or other representative other than the director has authority to enter into any agreement for employment for any specified period and that any employment with the organization will be at will and may be terminated at any time for any reason by either the organization or by me. I also understand that this application and any employment manuals or handbooks that may be distributed to me during the course of my employment shall not be construed as a contract.

DATE: _____ SIGNATURE: _____

Form revised December 12, 2007

APPENDIX B

Application Rating Form for Museum Education and Tour Coordinator Candidates

Name of person rating applications: _____

Date of rating: _____

Education
5 = master's degree or above in related field
4 = bachelor's degree in related field
3 = master's degree in unrelated field
2 = bachelor's degree in unrelated field
1 = neither

Work Experience (based on full-time years of work experience)
7 = three or more years of history museum/historic site education experience
6 = three or more years of art/science/etc. museum education experience
5 = three or more years of history museum/historic site experience without education component
4 = three or more years of art/science/etc. museum experience without education component
3 = three years of education experience without museum experience
2 = less than three years museum/historic site or education experience
1 = no related work experience

Experience in Planning and Implementing Education Programs, Tours, and Special Events
5 = three or more years of experience
4 = two or more years of experience
3 = one or more years of experience
2 = experience in these areas as an intern or volunteer
1 = no apparent experience in these areas

APPENDIX B

Writing and Computer Abilities

5 = excellent writing skills and apparent computer skills, including Dreamweaver

4 = average to good writing skills and apparent computer skills

3 = fair to average writing skills and unknown computer skills

2 = below average writing skills and apparent computer skills

1 = below average writing skills and no computer skills or unknown

Volunteer and Intern Supervision and Training Experience

5 = extensive experience with recruiting, supervising, and training volunteers and interns

4 = extensive experience with volunteers but not with interns

3 = extensive experience with interns but not with volunteers

2 = some experience in these areas

1 = no experience listed in these areas

Quality of Presentation

Did the candidate follow the instructions in the website posting?

Is the cover letter well written? Are there typos or grammatical errors? Does it follow business letter format?

Is the resume presented professionally and well organized?

5 = excellent

4 = above average

3 = average

2 = below average

1 = major deficiencies

Number	Education	Work Experience	Program, Tour, and Event Planning Experience	Writing and Computer Skills	Volunteer/ Intern Supervision Experience	Quality of Presentation	Add One Bonus Point If Candidate Has Oberlin History Knowledge	Total
1								
2								
3								
4								
5								

My top three rated candidates are as follows:

	Number	Comments
1		
2		
3		

APPENDIX C

Employee Evaluation Form

Name: _____   Date of Evaluation: _____

Rating Scale:
4 = Strong
3 = Satisfactory
2 = Needs Improvement
1 = Unsatisfactory

Performance Factors	Rating
Production/quantity of work (produces the expected amount of work)	
Thoroughness/accuracy/quality of work (gets the job done right)	
Dependability/independent action (uses initiative, is reliable, does not require close supervision)	
Work methods (works efficiently, plans ahead, is organized, flexible, and able to manage multiple tasks)	
Problem solving (analyzes relevant facts, makes sound recommendations)	
Interpersonal skills (works well with supervisor, staff, and volunteers, is respectful, cooperative, and visitor/ customer oriented)	
Written communication (clear, well organized, grammatically correct, efficient, well presented)	
Communication with supervisor (follows instructions, keeps supervisor informed)	
Job knowledge (proficient in methods or skills required and acquiring knowledge)	
Work habits (has good attendance, does not allow personal calls or discussions to interfere with or disrupt work)	

APPENDIX C

Performance Factors	Rating
Appearance (wears professional attire, is well groomed, creates a positive impression for the organization)	
Attitude (situationally appropriate, matched to task)	
Suitability for a museum position and multitask environment	
Ability to work in accordance with mission, core values, policies, and procedures	

Overall Rating:

Discussed with employee on _____.

Signature of Supervisor: _____ Date: _____

Signature of Employee: _____ Date: _____

INDEX

letter, 96–97; projects, 88; questions
for college coordinators, 90; questions
to consider regarding, 87; record
keeping, 106–7; revamping/starting,
86–97; successful, 107–8; unlikely, 88;
unpaid, 81
interviews: hiring process, 49–50; intern,
93, 95–96; security contractor, 14
IPM. *See* integrated pest management
IUPUI. *See* Indiana University–Purdue
University Indianapolis

job descriptions, 38–42; abilities, 92;
application requirements, 93; contents,
38; details in, 91, 93; for interns,
90–93; Oberlin Heritage Center
(examples), 39–40, 41–42; positions
available, 92; sample, 92–93; skills,
92–93; volunteer, 40–42

key program, 14
Klingler, Stacy, xii

leaks, *13*
legal concerns, 74–75
liability: insurance, 23–24; volunteer, 74
lifelong learning, 72
lighting safety, 12–13
Lynden Pioneer Museum, 45, 47

Magnes Collection of Jewish Art and
Life, 43–44; mission, 43
maintenance: collections, 8; cyclical,
9–10; funding, 12; garden, 7; periodic,
7; preventative, 7–8; regular, 4–5, 7;
security system, 10
MAP. *See* Museum Assessment Program
master key, 14
Mature Services, Inc., 47
MayDay, 20–21
McCain, Dan, 46–47
McGuire, Amanda, 107
Merrill Associates Topic of the Month,
78

Minnesota Historical Society
Housekeeping Handbook, 8
mission, 111; facility use related to, 26–
27; Magnes Collection of Jewish Art
and Life, 43; volunteers supporting,
68
Morris, Susan S., 43–44
Morris-Butler House Museum, 81, 86,
87, 103, 107
Museum Assessment Program (MAP),
56, 111; Oberlin Heritage Center, 57
Museum-Ed, 78
Museum-L, 78
Museum magazine, 55

name tags, 34
National Endowment for the Humanities
(NEH), 56; Consultant Grant, 120
National Volunteer Week, 73
NEH. *See* National Endowment for the
Humanities
New York Council for the Humanities
(NYCH), 121
New York State Council on the Arts
(NYSCA), 120
Noble County Historical Society, 81, 86,
87–88, 103, 108
Nonprofit World, 56
Norris, Linda, 120, 121
North Star Museum of Boy Scouting and
Girl Scouting, 11, 26; circuit maps, *6*;
operations manual, *5*
NYCH. *See* New York Council for the
Humanities
NYSCA. *See* New York State Council on
the Arts

Oberlin Heritage Center, 47;
accreditation, 58; awards and
celebrations at, *33*; employment
application, 123–27; fact sheet, 35;
field trips, *55*; holiday brunch, *33*; job
descriptions, 39–40, 41–42; MAP, 57;
volunteer application form, 69

Ohio Association of Historical Societies and Museums, *33*
Ohio Historical Society, 47
Ontario County Historical Society, 120–21
operations manual: assembling, 3; facility manager keeping, 3; keeping up to date, 3; North Star Museum of Boy Scouting and Girl Scouting, 5; suggested contents, 4
organic material inspections, 11
orientation strategy, 52
Ott, Margaret, 87–88, 102, 108
outside speakers, 55

parking lot: permeable surfaces on, 12; plowing, 5, 7
partnerships. *See* collaboration
peer review, 56
performance issues, 54
personnel manual: attorney review, 36; fact sheet as base for, 61n1; sections, 36–37; transparency, 38; volunteer manual adapted from, 36
preventative maintenance, 7–8
private funding, 109–10
professional development, 54–56

recession, 109
records retention and destruction policy, 52
references: hiring process, 50; interns, 95–96
rental: facility, 2, 24–27; policy considerations, 27
Retired Senior Volunteer Program, 68
Rice County Historical Society, *20*
risk assessments, 17–18
roof inspections, 9
routing slip, 55

safety/security, 1–2, 12–21; accident/incident reporting, 21; cameras, 15; cases, 16; collections management as,

18; contractor interviews, 14; disaster planning, 18–21; lighting and, 12–13; local, 14; lockdown drills, 17; risk assessment, 17–18; staff and, 15
salary surveys, 40
Sarbanes-Oxley legislation, 56
Schweinfurth Memorial Art Center, 119–20
security system: access levels, 15; customizing, 14–15; disarming, 15; electronic, 14; false alarms, 14–15; logs, 15; maintenance, 10; phone lines disabled and, 15; testing, 10
self-assessments, 111; employee, 53
Seminar for Historical Administration, 56
Seward House, 117–20
sexual predators, 70
Singer, Herb, 43–44
skaters, 23
Small Museums Administrators Committee, 56
Small Museums Committee, xii
Society for Nonprofit Organizations, 56
staff: defined, 1; enacting policies, 63; security and, 15–16; visitors threatening, 16; volunteers performing key functions of, 45–47. *See also* docent; interns; volunteers
standards, 57–59; principle areas, 58
Standards and Excellence Program for History Organizations (StEPs), 57, 111
The Standards for Excellence: An Ethics and Accountability Code for the Nonprofit Sector, 58
student: interns, 82–83; supervision, 82; volunteers, 68; work experience, 82
Summer in the Finger Lakes, 120–21; budget of, 121

teamwork, 31–36; goal, 32; thanking and, 32
thanking, 32; teamwork and, 32; volunteers, 73

ABOUT THE EDITORS

Cinnamon Catlin-Legutko has worked in the small museum world since 1994 and was the director of the General Lew Wallace Study & Museum in Crawfordsville, Indiana, from 2003 to 2009. In 2008, the museum was awarded the National Medal for Museum Service. Her contributions to the field include leadership of the AASLH Small Museums Committee, service as an IMLS grant reviewer and AAM MAP peer reviewer, and service as an AASLH Council member. She is now CEO of the Abbe Museum in Bar Harbor, Maine.

Stacy Klingler currently serves local history organizations as the assistant director of local history services at the Indiana Historical Society. She began her career in museums as the assistant director of two small museums, before becoming director of the Putnam County Museum in Greencastle, Indiana. She chairs the AASLH's Small Museums Committee (2008–2012) and attended the Seminar for Historical Administration in 2006. While she lives in the history field, her passion is encouraging a love of learning in any environment.

ABOUT THE CONTRIBUTORS

Claudia J. Nicholson has thirty years of experience in history museums and historical agencies, as well as a master's degree in history museum studies from the Cooperstown Graduate Program. An experienced curator, she became executive director, fundraiser, curator, educator, press officer, and tour guide at the North Star Museum of Boy Scouting and Girl Scouting in North St. Paul, Minnesota, in 2005. Her chapter was written based on her experience converting a non-purpose-built structure into a history museum.

Patricia Anne Murphy is the first executive director of the Oberlin Heritage Center. She has a bachelor's degree in history from Grinnell College and a master's in architectural history from the University of Virginia. She is a graduate of the Seminar for Historic Administration and the Getty Museum Leadership Institute and is a Certified Fund Raising Executive. She serves on the American Association of Museums Accreditation Commission and is the past president of the Ohio Association of Historical Societies and Museums/Ohio Local History Alliance.

Patricia L. Miller is the executive director of the Illinois Heritage Association, a nonprofit service organization based in Champaign, Illinois. She works with museums, libraries, and other cultural heritage organizations throughout the state. A peer reviewer for the American Association of Museums for its Accreditation and Museum Assessment programs, Miller is an adjunct lecturer in the history department at Eastern Illinois University, Charleston, where she has taught graduate classes in historic site administration since 1985.

Amanda Wesselmann is associate director of the General Lew Wallace Study & Museum. She has supervised and trained volunteers and interns for over seven years. She has worked in almost all areas of the museum field over the past nine years, including education, volunteer coordination, exhibit fabrication, collections, development, and administration. As associate director, Wesselmann coordinates recruiting, training, and supervising volunteers; oversees educational programs and special events; and assists in traditional administrative duties.

Eileen McHugh has been the executive director of the Cayuga Museum of History and Art in Auburn, New York, since 2000. The Cayuga Museum, also home to the Case Research Laboratory, has a dual focus on local history and the invention of sound film. McHugh, a believer in her museum as a center of community engagement, has been very successful in raising its profile through a focus on family-friendly programming and diversifying exhibition themes.